MISS NANCY, UNCLE LARRY, AND A LIZARD NAMED KATHY

BETSY NOONAN AND DAVID STRATSO

ISBN 978-1-64492-134-0 (paperback)
ISBN 978-1-64492-135-7 (digital)

Christian Faith Publishing, Inc.
832 Park Avenue
Meadville, PA 16335
www.christianfaithpublishing.com

Printed in the United States of America

Dedicated
to my husband John
and
My Family
For their unfailing support over the years

INTRODUCTION

Why was this story written? Of what interest could it be to others? What does the silly title mean? It began as a family exercise to record the many anecdotes involving a small boy, which evolved into something more. This story is the journey of a young man from infancy to contributing adult and the mother who got him there. This alone may not seem remarkable. In this case, there were numerous medical issues afflicting this child born to a young unprepared mother. Any one of the obstacles they faced could have derailed this young life, sentencing him to an unproductive existence with limited educational or vocational opportunities.

Why did it not happen? That is a major part of this story. There is a lesson in these lives and those who joined the journey with them. Some will share their experiences. Others will have their contribution highlighted throughout. We hope the reader will learn what we continually have known: what this family experienced through their enduring faith is nothing short of remarkable.

When infants are born normal and healthy to parents with the means to raise a child, one could pretty much anticipate the child should expect a productive life. What if the infant child is born with numerous physical issues to a young mother without means? If such a mother feels deflated, lacking in courage, or otherwise is overwhelmed with the responsibility, what might happen to her child?

Betsy, son *Scott*, adoptive father *John Noonan*, with an extended family embracing them, would not submit. They would, instead, make any sacrifice to provide a normal life for Scott, including challenging educational opportunities, many life experiences, and the chance to be just like any other boy. They later would be joined by two more sons, *Blake* and *Joshua*.

5

Scott was born with *Goldenhar syndrome*. It will be helpful to have a brief understanding of this condition before joining the journey. *Goldenhar syndrome* is congenital, causing certain abnormalities in the formation of the face, head, and spine. It is a rare disease, occurring in about 1 out of 25,000 babies. No known cause, hence unpreventable as of this writing. For people with this syndrome, abnormalities appear mostly in the areas of the ears, eyes, and spine. This condition can affect the structure of the face and some internal organs. The severity of the abnormalities and symptoms varies by individual. Other than deformed ears, Scotty did not appear to have other issues as a newly born infant.

As he grew, other conditions surfaced, requiring numerous corrective surgeries, the most traumatic surgery being the insertion of steel rods to the front and back in a spinal fusion. This particular procedure was an attempt to diminish the onset of scoliosis. The result of this surgery meant his height would be compromised and restrict head and neck movement.

The lesson here is not extraordinary. It is simply to maintain one's faith and *not* surrender to bad circumstances. It takes perseverance and prayer while remaining hopeful. The mother and little boy never accepted his condition as limiting his opportunities to excel. In all aspects, he never believed he was different nor limited. Time has proven him right.

These brief experiences provided by Scott's maternal grandparents and Betsy's two sisters, Nancy and Cynthia, provide a sense of his personality. It is a good place to begin.

> *Blessed is the one who perseveres under trial because, having stood the test, that person will receive the crown of life the Lord has promised to those who love him. (James 1:12)*

FAMILY EXPERIENCES

Grandmother Mary Lu: Scooter, Scotty, Scott

Where do I begin? Our first grandchild, Scotty, was born January 22, 1987. There was much happiness and excitement anticipating his arrival. After his birth, our lives changed dramatically. Throughout his life, we experienced deep emotional pain for all Scotty had to endure. At the same time, we experienced much joy, happiness, and pleasure. We were truly blessed to have him in our lives. From Grandma's point of view, he was and still is amazing. God gave us a miracle gift, and we have been forever grateful.

I will never forget going to Riverside Hospital to see our daughter, Betsy, after Scotty was born. As I got off the elevator and looked down the hallway toward the nursery, I could see her peering through the nursery window. Betsy was leaning with her head against the window. As I got closer, I began to see her face. My heart broke, as I could see her sadness and despair reflected in the nursery window. I could tell that the reality of an unbelievable responsibility had set in. She certainly had to be worried about how she would manage. Although married, there was not going to be a long partnership in caring for this newborn. The burden on the marriage was too great, and within a couple of years, it dissolved.

After his birth, there were so many unanswerable questions: Why was he born with this Goldenhar syndrome? Where do we go from here? What would be his potential? How will he converse or interact with others? And these were the obvious questions. With an abundance of God's blessings and tons of family support, we got through every challenge and every obstacle. But it took lots of prayers and faith.

One of my most special times with Scotty was when Dave, his grandfather, and I would babysit him. If I was sitting on our love seat in the sunroom, he would hop on my lap, grab one of my arms to wrap around him, and cuddle. It was genuine affection on his part. He was too young to know there were rewards for making me melt with love. To the present, he has always been attentive to his grandpa and grandma and sensitive to our needs.

Betsy was amazingly resilient and resourceful during those early years. Scotty demonstrated a personality of accepting whatever the challenge was—no fear. As emotionally strong as he was, there was still the little boy in him trying to figure out what was happening. His communication skills accelerated as he grew and benefited from hearing aids and therapy. He was the most affable, engaging little boy I have ever known.

He endured numerous corrective surgeries, and as the number mounted, he became more hesitant and reluctant to endure more discomfort and pain. In addition to the actual surgeries, there were visits to the Cleveland Clinic for presurgery consultation, testing, and follow-up visits. Dave and I helped by taking Scotty to the clinic as often as needed. Since Betsy was working, we wanted to help her avoid losing time and money.

One such visit, when Scotty was eight years old, we took him for a routine follow-up with a specialist at the clinic. It was a two-hour-drive one way. For Betsy, it was more like an hour and a half. Scotty was an avid reader. In the daylight, on the way over to Cleveland, he would read. Scotty not only read, but he also consumed and retained information. During the ride, it was like he was not there: meaning the backseat was quiet. However, in the winter, on the ride home, it would be too dark for him to read. "Chatty" Scotty would surface as soon as we hit the road for home.

One particular ride home, he and Grandpa got into a sports trivia contest that lasted longer than we would have thought. One contest was Dave giving Scotty the name of a university, and Scotty would tell us the school's mascot/nickname. It became a fun game as the miles flew by. Scotty never hesitated or missed a beat in responding correctly. Sometimes Dave had to accept Scotty was right because he could not contest the answer provided. Scotty was remarkable with his knowledge. Dave had more trouble thinking of universities than Scotty had in giving the answer.

Dave quietly said to me, "I've got to get this kid. I'll come up with one a little more obscure he likely won't know." Dave would not know either, but that did not matter. We only needed Scotty to admit he did not have an answer. A couple of miles rolled by before Dave shouted back to Scotty, "Massachusetts!" Silence in the backseat followed by, "No fair making them up, Grandpa!" The final score was lopsided in favor of Scotty. His trivia knowledge was not limited to college football and basketball. He followed all sports and knew all sorts of statistics, including betting odds and point spreads.

Around this same period in Scotty's life, Betsy met a caring, devoted young man with the solid character it would take to become involved in their lives. John embraced Scotty and was quick to share he fell in love with Scotty before he did Betsy. One day, he asked if he could visit. We were both a little concerned and curious as to why he wanted to visit alone with us. Dave had no clue what John's intent was when he asked to visit. Mom's intuition meant I had a hunch. After some awkward small talk, John formally asked for our permission to ask Betsy to marry him. A good example of his character: he sought our blessing and permission. I excitedly jumped up and yelped, "Yes!" Dave, on the other hand, being his more practical self, stayed seated and asked, "Why?"

With their marriage, Scotty acquired a caring father who could support and guide his development. A father, two additional grandparents, and a whole new bunch of relatives to embrace him.

When Scotty was ten years old, he underwent a horrific procedure involving the spine. This particular operation was performed at the Shriner's Children's Hospital in Chicago and was described as risky and tedious. It was a twelve-hour nightmare, shared by Betsy, John, and John's cousin, Father Jim Halleron. Fr. Jim had driven over from Mansfield, Ohio, the morning of the surgery. And of course, Dave and me. We were all in the waiting room the entire time. When the surgery was finally complete, only Grandma was on duty. Being left alone was frightening for ole Grandma. We quickly gathered everyone. The chief surgeon shared the results with all of us.

After several days, we were able to actually visit with Scotty. I knew he wanted a number 45 football jersey of one of his heroes at the time, Andy Katzenmoyer, the star linebacker for the Ohio State University. I vowed to get one for him no matter the effort. I telephoned a collegiate store near OSU's campus. Remarkably, the store had one left in his size, and it was mailed out the same day. Scotty was unable to communicate for a while because of his sedated condition and all the tubes, etc. I asked him if he could hear me, and he squeezed my hand. I was greatly moved and relieved. I shared with him the jersey would be coming within the week. I could see the excitement in his eyes.

Since he was in the children's hospital for a considerable time, Dave and I did not remain with Betsy and John the entire period. Several days later, Dave and I returned to Chicago with the jersey in hand. The jersey could not alleviate the discomfort he still felt, but it did a lot to improve his morale. He was feeling better enough to make a request. On our next visit, he wanted us to bring him some of Dave's collection of the Three Stooges videos. Those silly things actually provoked giggles from this little body all wrapped in a body brace.

Each surgery was an encounter for Betsy, John, and Scotty—frequently shared by Dave and me. Except for clipping his tongue, all of his surgeries required extended hospital stays. Hospital stays became a real agonizing experience for him. He hated being in the hospital. At one of his final less-serious surgeries at the Cleveland Clinic, the surgeon assured Scotty he would be able to go home right after the surgery.

While I was sitting alone with him in recovery, he began coming out of the anesthetic. Immediately, when he became aware of his circumstances, he bolted upright, looked around, and began pulling out IVs and anything else attached to him. No one ever shared with him he would have to remain in recovery for a couple of hours before he would be discharged.

He caught me off guard with how quickly he recovered. I was in a panic as I shouted and grabbed at Scotty, "No! Lie back down and leave those things alone." He started to sob, insisting he had been told he would be able to go home immediately after the surgery. It made no difference to him his actions were causing pain. He wanted to get everything out and off him so he could go home.

We frequently were entrusted with caring for him for brief periods. He was never ever a problem. We would go for walks, and he would chatter away. The word "silence" was unknown to Scotty. It was a concept that eluded him. We took him to various places or venues, such as the circus, movies, parks, concerts. You name it, we did it. One time, we went to Cedar Point with our entire extended family. We were dismayed by the number of stares he received. A little girl was staring at him, along with her siblings and parents. Scotty neither noticed, nor would he have been fazed by it. Protective Grandma approached them. "May I help you with something?" I gave them a stern look as I said it. All in all, people were pretty sensitive to and accepting of his issues.

From an early age, he seemed to set goals. Many were unattainable, but he tried. He did manage to play Little League baseball for a few years, which gave the whole family entertaining afternoons. He had an eclectic taste in music, which extended to older masters such as B. B. King. In 1996, the King came to Toledo, and Dave and I made sure Scotty was in the audience. He surely had to be the only nine-year-old true fan in the audience. He bopped and sang along. It was always fun and entertaining to be in Scotty's company.

His goal setting remained with him. One of his more amusing modest goals, to which we could all contribute, was becoming the owner of thirty pairs of boxer shorts. Being away at college meant doing his own laundry. He had reasoned he would have to do laundry only once a month if he had that many boxers. It became a big deal to him.

Our family physician for a number of years was Dr. Joe Schneider. He attended to Scotty's general health issues with great care and sensitivity. He summed up Scotty's life in one simple sentence: "He is a lesson to all of us." Scotty has always been polite and extremely caring. Being attentive to grandparents and his extended family is his nature. I believe it is his way to be so loving, but much credit goes to the nurturing of his mother, Betsy.

Grandfather Dave

My first memory of my grandson was Scotty being rocked by his grandmother, Mary Lu, after he was born. Her face was beaming as she held her first grandchild. The excitement could not hide our concerns for his mild-appearing deformity. We both had grave concerns as to what this meant for the future. How would our young daughter deal with all the demands of a new baby with some physical issues we had yet to fully understand? What were his issues, and how bad could this be? How would the rest of our family react? How would I personally accept what, initially, seemed as a tragic story in the making? There was no denying he was incredibly cute in a sort of Popeye's "Swee'Pea" kind of way.

Not knowing the full extent of his condition, nor how he would be able to function, could this little life survive what all the world would be throwing at him? Although our concerns never left, we effortlessly grew attached to this little one who would soon be anointed, "Scooter." His birth name was Scott, but Scooter seemed a good fit, and sometimes Scoot. At least until he was old enough to go to school when he evolved into Scotty. When he got older, he preferred Scott. Family still calls him Scooter, occasionally. He was a typical infant: crying when hungry and pooping and peeing whenever he felt like it.

Becoming doting grandparents was easy because he was ours and, as we would soon know, a true gift from God. Early feelings, I must confess, were mostly negative. What did we do to deserve this? Would he even live beyond infancy? As weeks turned into months, and months into years, we knew we had been blessed with someone special and unique. All it ever took was his little face lighting up in a grin.

The other truly remarkable occurrence was witnessing our daughter blossom as she took command and became the consummate grizzly bear mother. Our whole family circled the wagons and embraced this newest member. Quite simply, he brought joy. His grandmother, Mary Lu, was especially loving and accepting of this little guy. As he grew, an amiable good-natured personality began peeking through. There was competition to hold him. Still, with all the joy, concern remained as we kept watching for signs of other impairments. In his early months, it was not clear how well he could see or hear.

If ever a small child could demonstrate unconditional love, it would be Scooter. Betsy's life with her husband was rocky, and money was scarce with neither having decent employment. When those conflicts eventually resulted in her becoming a single mom who had to work, Scooter experienced day care.

One particular late afternoon, I had to take Betsy to get Scooter from day care. As we entered the playroom where he normally spent his day, we could see him across the room sitting in a sort of Johnny Jump Up contraption. He was hanging with no movement and staring at nothing. Arms hanging limply along his little body. It was still unclear how well he might hear. Plus with weak eyesight, what could he see? Not until his surgeries years later would I ever witness anything more heartbreaking. As we got closer, he caught sight of Betsy and began bouncing. His face brightened with a grin filling his entire little face.

Now, some thirty years later, I can still see that smiling face. His little smile was an indication of what his personality would be like. He became inquisitive, engaging, fearless, affable, and extroverted. He was rarely quiet and seldom still. Not in an ADHD way. Scooter just needed to be involved with life.

At the time Scooter was born, I was working in an office in a skyscraper building in downtown Toledo. After Betsy went back to work as a single mom, we would sometimes have lunch together. Periodically, Betsy would appear at my office door. Her cheerful mask always hid the sadness she most certainly was experiencing. She only came to my office if she was in desperate need of some money. The ritual was pretty much the same. Some small talk, and then the request for $20. In buying power then, it was worth twice that amount in today's world. Still, I sometimes wish I had given her more. Given the tales I would tell and her periodic visits, our office staff and my boss got to know her and the whole story involving Scotty.

One day, she came by only to find I was in a meeting. How deflating it must have been for her. My caring boss quickly offered, "How much do you need?" He knew I would repay him.

When I reflect on those early years, a number of precious and amusing memories of my time with Scooter come to mind as he evolved to Scotty. He was a frequent guest with Mary Lu and me; that is, we were babysitters. Sometimes overnight. We enjoyed having Scooter around, and he was comfortable roaming our entire house. It was never dull or quiet, and we were always onstage for whatever the next challenge would be. One morning, when he was four, he wandered into our bathroom as I was drying off from my shower. I did not pay any attention until he passed by me, saying, "How you doing, Gramps," slapping my "Mr. Johnson" on his way out. No comment or reaction from him, as though it was nothing more than swatting at a low tree branch.

When he was about eight, I took him to the circus. It was not one of the modern indoor fancy-affairs circuses have become. We were in a big old tent in an open field outside of town. One needs to reflect on what it might have been like. Matted grass with a misty dew on it, with a barnyard-like aroma. This circus was one level above rundown. I half expected to see the lady performers in fishnet hosiery with patches on them. It had rickety bleachers with every imaginable cheap souvenir for sale, along with the ever-present popcorn and cotton candy, all of which he asked for and got from a compliant grandfather. At one point, though, I believed he had gotten enough junk and food. I did not want to overindulge him. Back came the vendors with balloons on a stick. By now, all the people around us had been witnessing this animated hyper small boy hounding his grandfather for stuff.

As soon as Scooter caught sight of the balloons, he said, "I want one of those." I quietly declined, stating he had gotten enough stuff. One needs to understand that to Scooter, hearing "no" is far from final. He will ask again and keep asking. And he did keep at it. So did my "no's." However, my voice and tone kept increasing in volume. Finally, he sort of groaned, spun around, and folded his arms in disgust. We had become part of the entertainment for those around us. I could sense the eyes of those close enough to have followed Scooter's continual asking for items. They, likely, were watching to see how this standoff was going to play out.

Sitting several seats from us was a pleasant young Asian man. He was engaging enough, though his English was not strong. A little girl in front of him was pressing her parents to get her a balloon. It was no easy task to maneuver out of our seating and the dozen or so steps to get a balloon. And that was the father's reason for not getting her a balloon. It would not have been a problem for me. Scooter was uninhibited and loved to do things for himself. If I had agreed to a balloon, he simply would have taken the money, run down the steps, and caught the guy selling the balloons.

What happened next was impressive and somewhat defeating. Our Asian neighbor spoke quietly to the little girl, stood, and excused his way along our row to the aisle. He purchased a balloon and returned, excusing his way back to his seat. He only got as far as our seats. Scooter grabbed his arm and said, "Can I have that one?" The young man was caught by surprise, hesitated a moment, smiled, and gave the balloon to Scooter. I did not even have time to protest and hung my head as the crowd all around us broke into laughter and applause. The young man turned, went back for another one, after graciously refusing payment for the one he had given Scooter.

The next summer, I took Scooter and his two close-in-age cousins, Corey and Kyle, to a Toledo Mud Hens game. It was the Hens former venue at the Lucas County fairgrounds. The three of them presented a challenge, with dollar signs attached. The venue was fairly small and the stands compact. It was safe to let them roam along the fences and dugouts. They were never out of sight. Of course, popcorn, cotton candy, hot dogs, candy, soft drinks, and more popcorn were their treats. I did finally draw the line, only not soon enough.

Corey and Kyle were more controlled in their intake and suffered no ill effects. I got a frantic phone call from Betsy, "Dad, what

15

did you feed Scooter?" When I asked why, she said he had been throwing up soon after my dropping him off at home. And it was green nasty stuff. I considered it to be a successful outing with three of my grandsons.

Some of my best moments as Scooter's grandfather came when it was the two of us going to the Cleveland Clinic. He was seven, eight, and nine for these trips. In those days, no law existed prohibiting a child his age and size from sitting in the passenger seat. He would have a rapid-fire litany of questions as we traveled the turnpike. The questions were interrupted frequently, only because he began talking about something else. The point is, he was never quiet—except when he was reading.

The drive to Cleveland for one late afternoon appointment was unremarkable because Scooter read. On the return trip, it was pitch black with a blinding blizzard snowstorm. It was so bad I believed it best to pull off in one of the service plazas to wait for the weather to improve. It would have been far too hazardous to pull off to the side of the highway. I still had to drive about thirty more miles to reach the next plaza. It became tense for me as I tried to focus to see through the swirling snow. It was dark, so Scooter did not have enough light to read. Which meant he would be talking, question after question on trivial things. Normally, it would have been okay. With my need to concentrate, I quickly became annoyed.

I asked him harshly to be quiet. A simple request to anyone else—a source of curiosity to Scooter. Why was it necessary for him to be quiet? So I explained our predicament with the lousy driving conditions and that it would be helpful if he could sit quietly. I wish now I could have said those words to him nicely and expletive-free. Well, at least he was quiet for a while.

During one nice weather trip, I pulled into a turnpike plaza to get us something to drink. Scooter saw an ice cream truck parked off to the side of the parking area. Yep, now his preference was ice cream, and further, "give me the money, I want to get it myself." The serving window was a good five feet above ground level. No way would they be able to see this little guy nor could he give them the money or be handed a cone. Quite an argument ensued, which I eventually won, only because I threatened, "No ice cream."

On a subsequent visit, Mary Lu, Scooter, and I were required to stay overnight at the clinic's Gatehouse Hotel—the one for frugal guests. We had gone out to eat, and upon returning to the hotel, we got caught in a downpour. We parked, and I grabbed an umbrella for the thirty-foot walk to the vestibule entrance.

A half dozen steps and he tugged at my arm. "I want to hold the umbrella." I tried to explain he was too little, and Grandma and I could not walk all hunched over trying to stay dry. It was a short debate, ending in a compromise. I told him when we got to the entrance, he could take over command of the umbrella. Scooter tucked the collapsed umbrella under his arm as we entered the vestibule. The point stuck out a good foot or more in front of him and the same with the handle end. Perhaps a dozen or more people were crowded into the vestibule waiting for the rain to clear. Our entrance was announced by the umbrella banging the door and windows and jabbing some people as we entered. He informed everyone in a loud authoritative voice, "Hey, it's really raining out there!"

Scooter became a huge OSU Buckeye fan, in spite of his adoptive father, John, being a Notre Dame loyalist. Betsy had always been in the Buckeye camp and had a head start influencing his allegiance. The team under John Cooper during the 1990s experienced considerable success, making them easy to cheer for. During the 1998 season, the University of Toledo was on the Buckeyes' early schedule. It is difficult to get tickets for a game in the Horseshoe. Through UT friends, Betsy was able to get three tickets for her, Scooter, and me. It became Scooter's objective to add John Cooper's autograph to his collection—an extremely challenging task.

Way before game time, I took him from our seats to the field and walked over to the walkway through which the team would enter the playing field. We were actually on the running track that circled the playing field. If we were lucky, we might get a chance for an autograph. We stood off to the side, right at the edge of a section of seating. I was unsure how Scooter would get his opportunity with so much commotion at that spot.

A friendly young man standing beside us helped. He glanced at Scotty as I told him we hoped to get an autograph from Coach Cooper. He told us the routine. The players would stop close to where we were standing and wait for the signal to run onto the field. John Cooper would always come out with them and work his way to the front of the players. He told us they would be in position for three or four minutes. It was at that moment he suggested Scooter should make his move to Cooper and before the state troopers could intervene. He said to wait until he gave Scooter the signal to dash to Cooper. He further had told us how sensitive Cooper was, and he never refused to autograph a program offered to him. Scotty knew no fear and was outgoing enough I had no doubt he would worm his way through the players to get to Cooper.

The team came out of the locker room soon after we got our instructions. It unfolded as the young man had instructed. With the group of players standing on their giant redwood-like legs, it seemed an impossible task. Would a small body be able to squirm through to reach Cooper buried in the middle of a half-dozen players? The little guy barely came to the waist of some of the players surrounding the coach. We heard the man say, "Go!" At that point, I gave him a gentle, but urgent shove. He dashed right out, hesitating only to push star tailback Michael Wiley to the side. He grabbed Cooper by the arm and thrust up his program with a pen. Cooper glanced down with a barely noticeable grin, scribbled his signature, and gave it back to Scooter. He dashed back to us. What a grin graced his face as I rubbed his head through his OSU baseball cap. We gave the young man our sincere thanks and worked our way back to our seats.

Skip forward to the summer between his freshman and sopho-more years at Miami of Ohio University. By now, he had progressed to Scott. So much of Scooter and Scotty still remained a part of him. He invited me to take him to a Mud Hens baseball game. This time, the Toledo baseball team played in a new stadium in downtown Toledo.

Toward the end of the game, we were standing behind the low-er-level seats on the fan walkway. It was at ground level, giving us a head start to the parking lot. I glanced at the fans seated in the section in front of us and thought I recognized a girl who had been a good friend of Scott through grade school and high school. I pointed to where she was sitting and asked Scott if it was Mallory. He looked and said he did not believe it was. As I watched her, I became more certain. Scott still believed it was not. I suggested he text Mallory and ask if she was at the same ball game. He got a quick response: "Don't know where you are, dude, but I am on the beach in North Carolina."

I was surprised to be so mistaken. I suggested we wait at the top as the fans filed out. It would give us a closer view and see if the young lady would recognize Scott. As soon as she reached the top where we were standing, she yelled, "Scotty!" Well, question resolved—it was Mallory. After small talk, she and her boyfriend went on their way. I turned to Scott. "So who did you text?" Scott replied, "I have no idea." "Well, how many Mallorys do you know who you might text?" I asked. "I don't think I know any other Mallorys." I could not resist asking, "Well, if it was not Mallory, who did you text?" He had no clue, even after searching his address book. This episode is the kind of occurrence that so endears him to us.

Not all of my involvement with Scott was entertaining or amusing. On one clinic visit with Betsy when he was about six, it was necessary for them to inject him with a dye to illuminate areas for a CAT scan. I followed Betsy and Scooter as they were taken to a room for the injection. I stayed in the hall when they entered the room, and the door closed behind them.

After a minute or two, I heard Scooter screaming. I could hear Betsy doing her best to soothe and comfort him. Scream after scream kept rolling out of the room. They were having great difficulty finding a suitable vein and repeatedly stuck him with a needle. I could not take it. I walked away out of earshot to avoid having to listen to his pain.

On another occasion, they attempted a bone graft in his jaw in an attempt to work on keeping his face somewhat symmetrical. It meant taking a piece of bone from his rib and grafting it into his right jaw. It amounted to two surgical points. The procedure was uncomfortable, with both his rib and jaw having incisions.

The rib healed nicely, but the jaw became infected. The incision needed to be opened and left to heal from the inside out. So this poor little boy had to cope with the open wound until it healed. The worst part was Betsy had to deep cleanse the incision regularly. Imagine someone thrusting a finger into a deep cut. The discomfort to Scooter was excruciating. I know because Mary Lu and I helped Betsy perform the procedure. It meant sitting in a chair and wrapping my legs around his legs and my arms around his upper body, pinning his arms, while Mary Lu immobilized his head. Betsy was amazing, performing a task not many would have the courage to do or be capable of performing. Like other procedures, time healed the pain. It was a needless discomfort as the graft effort failed. I got off easy, as these were the only two difficult incidents I came in close contact. I was a direct witness to a caring mother treating and consoling her small child.

The above passages with Scott are so reminiscent of our life with him. We were so blessed God chose to give Scott to our family. I believe God knew we would love and nurture this young life and help him become a productive member of society. We furnished the support. However, it was Scott's engaging personality, his resilience, and his refusal to feel sorry for himself that helped him attain so much in his young life. Perhaps God gave him a personality enhanced with an endearing quality and extroverted style to compensate for his diminished hearing and eyesight. After watching all his antics and adventures over the years, it has been clear to me that his guardian angel is highly skilled with immense stamina. In fact, God, likely, may have assigned more than one angel. He has been an unending source of joy, laughter, tears, and pride, all mixed together. And that is life.

Aunt Nancy, aka Miss Nancy

The night Scotty was born, I recall my dad calling, "It's a boy, and apparently there is something wrong with his ears." From his tone, I could tell he was disturbed. At the same time worried, concerned, and confused about Scotty's overall condition.

The next evening, the rest of our family went to meet him. Oh yes, and to say hi to Betsy. When I got my first chance to hold him, I thought to myself, *"How incredibly beautiful he is."* I knew instantly I loved him. It was a warm sensation telling me everything would be fine. Scotty would be okay.

There was no way we were going to wait until Betsy brought him home from the hospital to see him again. We visited them in the hospital as often as we could sneak in. One evening after having visited with Betsy and baby, Mom, Dad, my sister Cynthia, and I left the hospital early to get a bite to eat before heading home. It was January, so there was snow, ice, and cold, cold darkness as we left.

We had all parked in the same pay lot, one of those you pay when you leave by dropping quarters into a slot. The gate should lift for the car to exit. We were in two cars, so Cynthia, a friend, and I left in one car with Mom right behind us. She had to swing by to get Dad, who had to wait at the hospital entrance. His leg was in a cast, and he was on crutches. It was too hazardous for him to try to walk to the car.

Well, we dropped the quarters in, the gate shuddered, made an effort to lift, and fell back in place. We made several attempts, all ending the same. The cold and ice must have prevented the mechanism from working. In the meantime, Mom was behind us wondering why we were not going. No cell phones, so some yelling back and forth. Dad, though, was waiting and shivering as badly as the gate. He had no clue what was wrong, and even from a distance, we could see him raise his crutches over his head, forming a Y, and shaking them in the air. We knew we were the only ones laughing, but were not bothered in the least. We knew Dad was thinking, *"What in the world is going on?"* We finally escaped the lot by having one of us stand outside of the car, physically force the gate, and hold it until both cars exited.

Our whole family was so thrilled to have an infant we could all embrace. Scotty's early physical issues proved to be only a minimal distraction. Within months, we saw only a cute little guy who showed early signs of having a playful personality. Once Betsy and Scotty were out of the hospital, we made sure all of us would visit my parents' home if we knew they would be visiting. Many times it was on Sunday.

When Scooter was about a year old, we were all together for Sunday dinner. As usual, it was Dad's spaghetti on the menu. Scooter had one of those baby seats that fastened to the table to make a high chair seat with a tray. Watching the little guy eat spaghetti with his hands was entertaining. His face soon was covered with sauce and some small strings of spaghetti.

Cynthia and I soon found Scooter mimicking any gesture we would make. The smiles and laughter quickly became part of our meal. His grins were infectious, so we kept thinking about what we could do to get him to laugh and follow along. After a quiet consultation with Cynthia, we agreed rubbing our hands in our hair and all over our heads should get the results we were after. Scooter's hands, of course, were covered with tomato sauce and bits of spaghetti. When he mimicked our hands rubbing our heads, he was painting his whole head with sauce. With conscious hand movement, we got Scooter to paint every spot on his head, all the time grinning at us. Although having fun with Scooter was the main attraction, we knew we were having fun with Betsy. We could see her groaning, realizing he was going to be a mess to clean.

I was so infatuated with Scotty I would take vacation days to babysit him. I could not wait to spend the day with him, all to myself. I believed it was a true honor to be asked to be his godmother. It was during these early years I became Miss Nancy.

I was Miss Nancy, not Aunt Nancy, for a brief time during Scotty's early years. Because of hearing issues, he did not fully understand some things like the word "aunt." His interpretation was *Miss Nancy*, which followed the way he addressed his day care workers. For some unknown reason, my husband, Greg, became *Uncle Larry*. It was one of Scotty's quirks that made him so endearing. This is how he knew us and is the way he addressed us. In time, he got the names and titles straight. It was amusing while it lasted.

My first child, Corey, was born shortly after Scooter's third birthday. At Corey's baptism following a Sunday Mass, Scotty became one of the star attractions on the video recording of the baptism.

The church was empty except for family. While we were all focused on the ceremony, my brother-in-law was video recording the event. When we viewed the film, we watched as the camera slowly panned left, moved away from the baptism, and zeroed in on Scooter. He was toward the middle of the empty church on the pews playing "Superman." His pants were rolled up, and he had fastened his coat as a cape. Bad guys were being wrestled into submission as he flew from the pew seats to the center aisle. A serious religious event was, for a time, upstaged by Scooter.

Later that year, my dad's mother, my grandmother, passed away after a long illness. She and my grandfather lived in my parents' hometown an hour away. It fell to Dad and his sister to make all the arrangements. Although an unhappy time, her death was not unexpected.

Our whole family gathered at the funeral home for the viewing. Scooter, of course, was front and center visiting with family and strangers alike. For him, it was another outing and chance to explore a new place. The funeral home had plush carpeting with a fancy scroll pattern. The pattern made it a little challenging for Scotty given his weak eyesight. Off to the side of one of the two sitting rooms was an eight-foot ramp dropping downhill about three feet, leading to the double doors of the embalming room. Protective railings were on either side of the drop-off, with the entry area open.

On one of his skipping excursions, Scotty got too close to the entry point of the ramp. The busy carpet design disguised the slanting drop-off. In an instant, he was rolling down the ramp and crashing into the double doors, knocking them wide open, exposing the prep area and caskets. Greg, aka Uncle Larry, was on him in a flash, lifting him by his midsection like a piece of luggage. Too late to prevent the noise of the banging of the doors and those of us giving controlled screams.

Despite the somberness of the occasion, it was difficult to suppress our laughter. Those who witnessed the tumble, including my dad, could not stifle their laughter. This was a true "Scooter" moment. He was totally unaffected by the mishap, trotting off as though nothing unusual had taken place. It was an awkward period while we regained our composure.

All the entertaining moments helped provide balance to the difficult times Scotty had to endure. We were watching a disadvantaged young boy overcome the odds and grow into a contributing adult. He has always earned our respect and admiration for how he has endured and has lived his life.

Aunt Cynthia

I have heard something like it takes a village to raise a child. So it was not unusual for someone in the family to be watching Scotty while he was growing up. Although I was sixteen, I had babysat other people's children only a handful of times. So when it was my turn to watch Scotty at my parents' home, I was a bit uneasy doing it by myself. My dad was home, so I enlisted his help. Two-year-old Scotty was an extremely active little toddler. Curious, playful, and adventurous as they come. He could not be left alone for even a moment.

I had Scotty upstairs with me while I was watching him. Our upstairs housed my bedroom and a loft separated by a short catwalk overlooking the downstairs foyer. Although my dad was in the loft with us, Scotty was my responsibility. My sixteen-year-old mind knew that stairs around Scotty is a pretty bad idea. So I was especially watchful. I knew keeping him within arm's reach was the only way to handle such a situation. Even being vigilant, he still managed to escape me and ran as fast as his little legs could go along the catwalk, heading right toward the stairs. Scotty, even at this stage of life, thought he could do what anyone else could do and knew no fear.

Panic immediately set in, and I screamed for my dad who quickly joined me. We both knew what was about to happen, and neither of us could do anything about it. I was terrified. This little peanut of a boy in my care was about to tumble down the stairs. He could be seriously injured, if not worse. At a minimum, he could break something on his already fragile little body. This little boy already was destined to have many physical challenges ahead of him in his life. I felt it would be my fault if he has to endure an unnecessary injury.

All these horrible thoughts were racing through my mind in a split second. I could not reach him, I could not grab him, and I could not save him from this fall. At the next moment, it happened. Scotty stepped off the catwalk onto the stairs, as if he was on a level floor. My father and I both felt helpless, not able to do anything but watch. We both watched in horror as he tumbled down the stairs. Like a slinky toy effortlessly flipping over and over, Scotty went head over heels…tumbling like a gymnast would do cartwheels…all the way to the bottom. What have I permitted to happen? How would I explain this to my sister?

The tumble seemed endless. My stomach was doing flips with every one of his tumbles. What felt like forever finally came to a dramatic conclusion. We both rushed down to Scotty's aid, ready to help him, console him, kiss him, and tell him it was going to be okay. To our amazement, Scotty rolled off the last step and landed standing on his feet. He was facing the stairs with his sweet dimpled hands resting on the first step. He paused momentarily and casually trotted off toward the kitchen, likely to see if anything interesting was going on with Grandma.

Our curious, playful, and adventurous Scotty was perfectly fine. Given his personality, to him, his tumble was nothing scary, special, or extraordinary. His developing mind, likely, thought, *"Well, I wanted to get to the bottom, and I did."* Our panic was replaced immediately with relief. Potential tears and anguish instead became relief, astonishment, and laughter. This event, alarming in our minds, did not faze him one bit. To this day, my dad and I reflect on this tumble with giggles and sorry no one else got to witness it.

One summer when Scotty was three and a half years old, we all went to my mother's family reunion. This was the first get-together with her family in years. With Scotty's engaging and comical personality, we were unconcerned about how they would react to this little guy and his physical issues. It took only seconds for him to meet and endear himself with all of his distant relatives.

Between the parking area and the shelter house was a small creek with a short bridge used to cross over. Most of my mom's family were there already. While we were gathering our various food items, Betsy lifted Scotty out of the car and set him on the ground. With all the loud greetings coming from the shelter house, Scotty immediately took off to meet these new people. The fact a creek was between him and his new friends did not register in his young mind.

He covered the ten feet to the creek faster than Betsy could react. In a blink, he was standing ankle deep in the creek with his Scooter grin. Laughter erupted from the shelter house. Welcome to the family. Now came the tricky part. How to extricate him without others slipping in. For Scooter, it was now a game of catch me if you can. Once on dry land, his sneakers were removed and tied to a tree limb to dry—which took the balance of the visit. Whatever else was wet, he would have to wear. Betsy was used to commotions like this with Scotty. Her biggest fear had been his falling in the creek and getting his hearing aid damaged by the water.

One of my pleasant memories of an older Scooter was his driving his own little battery-operated Corvette convertible. It was fairly nice sized and could hold a passenger along with the driver. My parents kept the car in their garage for when Scotty would visit. Little gestures by Scotty made it apparent he closely observed adult behavior. It even had a car phone, which he would pretend to use as he was driving.

He would hop in the car and take off down the driveway. Since our home was on a cul-de-sac on a street with no outlet, there was no traffic to interfere with his driving. He would circle the cul-de-sac and return to the driveway repeatedly. His style and antics made watching him a delight. Scotty did not drive like a small child; he drove like an adult complete with gestures. Once under way, he would prop his right arm across the back of the passenger seat and drive with his left hand. It was entertaining to watch him at play.

Ages eight, nine, and ten were Scotty's "wonder" years: we wondered what he would do next to entertain or impress us. During those years, he got into reading. He believed he could read anything and made attempts at newspaper articles and adult periodicals. He was attempting to read words he had no clue what they meant nor make the appropriate pronunciation. He would use phonics as he understood it to be.

With so much family close by, we tried to celebrate everybody's birthday with a separate party. All would attend, and it was a great way to stay close. The number of birthday parties soon became eleven, then twelve, then thirteen, as new nephews joined Scotty, Corey, and Kyle. The entertainment for these parties was Scotty reading aloud each card's message. The laughter at his butchered pronunciations delivered in a hesitating monotone made it seem like stand-up comedy. None of our laughter and joking bothered him in the least as he simply persevered through the last card.

One incident during those "wonder" years provided the best evidence of how personable and accepted Scotty was. My new husband, Joe, and I had him for the day. We were attending a high school graduation party in Oak Harbor, a nice small town about forty-five minutes from Toledo. We were walking along a residential street when a car passed by. It slowed and a head popped out, yelling, "Hey, hi, Scotty!" Scotty gave a little wave in response. Here we were in a small town where even we did not know many people, but someone knew Scotty. He had no idea who it was, nor how the person knew him.

We have always believed Scotty's personality, along with the love and support of family, helped him flourish. His accomplishments have been impressive. He has become a family treasure.

Grandma Mary Lu and
New born Scotty

Scotty's First Christmas

Scotty's Second Christmas
"How do I look?"

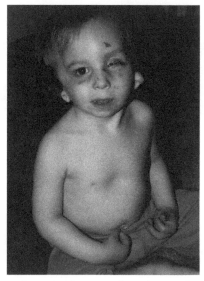

"You ought to see the other guy"

BETSY'S AND SCOTT'S STORY

The Beginning

To relate what transpired raising Scott in Toledo and Rossford, Ohio, meant having to reach back in memory to some dark days. Was it wise to examine old memories and old photos from the early days with Scott? It was an emotional time without much money and during which we faced many challenges over several years: one surgery and event leading to another. There were some amusing and fun times as well. We hoped by remembering and writing about all the fun times, it would offset those uncomfortable memories.

Scotty Is Born

As I lay in my hospital bed, I found myself staring out my window. There was nothing to stare at. It was winter; it was dark, and nothing was visible. I had never felt so alone. Even snow flurries would have been a welcome sight. Earlier in the day, I had given birth to a baby boy. What should have been an exciting time for my family and me had changed unexpectedly. I should have been waiting joyfully for a nurse to bring me my baby to feed. Instead, I was concerned as to how I would react when they placed little Scotty in my arms.

When Scotty was born on January 22, 1987, I did not ask whether it was a girl or a boy. I was more interested and worried about whether the baby was all right. I suppose it is an ongoing concern new mothers have. I had no insurance and little money, so when I became pregnant, I was seen in a clinic for poor and uninsured individuals. No prenatal testing, so I knew nothing about my baby until he was born. As they often do right after birth, they plopped Scotty on my chest. I heard the nurse mention deformed ears. Those words quickly got my full attention, shocking me fully conscious. Scotty was quickly whisked away, and the doctor and medical personnel took steps to reassure me.

I experienced a flood of emotions, and my mind was racing rapidly into the future. At that moment, I knew I had to grow up fast. I had turned twenty a short seven weeks earlier. My purpose immediately was clear. I had to love, guide, protect, and obtain the best medical care for my baby. Scotty's condition was a puzzle to the former Riverside hospital staff, so they called in a specialist from the Medical College of Ohio. They diagnosed Scotty as having Goldenhar syndrome. I was distraught and found it difficult to process what they were telling me. I did grasp the critical words describing the main problem areas. The ears were obvious.

The specialist, with his nurse, thoroughly explained the syndrome and all the other possible areas that could be affected. I was told what issues may surface later as Scotty grew. It was uncomfortable listening to all they were telling me, and it was difficult to grasp the enormity of the problem. It was too early to assess his eyesight and great concern over the level of hearing. Later testing would reveal the absence of a right inner ear, but the necessary structure was present in his left ear. There was a stubby growth for his right ear, more resembling an earlobe. His left ear was only partially formed.

With no internet, I could not research his condition on my own or learn about the experiences of others, but I was given some medical literature to help my understanding. No one could tell me why it happened to my baby nor help prepare me for the months and years ahead. While in the hospital, they performed a litany of diagnostic tests. We were relieved to learn that his body functions and heart seemed to be fine. At the time, it was believed that ears developed concurrently with the renal system. So if the ears did not form correctly, what would it mean about his kidney function? I prayed, "God, give me the strength I will need."

Being eager for any good news, I was greatly relieved when Scotty began peeing normally and showed no signs of renal failure. In addition to the problems of the syndrome, Scott's tongue was fastened to the base of his mouth, which meant I would be unable to breast-feed him. His initial feedings were by tube, progressing to "preemie" bottles. They kept Scotty for several days after I was discharged.

I was home now from the hospital, but hardly comfortable. I was sad, scared, and lonely. I was somewhat lonely because Scotty was not with me. I was back and forth to the hospital so I could spend time with my new baby. I spent as much time with him as the hospital would allow. I held him, rocked him, and fed him. He was soon discharged, and we were finally together 24/7. I had little help and got little sleep. All newborns require constant care, and Scotty was no different. I was petrified to have him out of my sight. I can still recall the soothing tick-ticking of the wind up swing I would put him in to keep him close to me.

However, my six-week maternity leave was not spent at home bonding with my newborn. Instead, weeks were filled with visit after visit with numerous specialists and testing. I believe Scotty was a curiosity and opportunity for the medical community to expand their knowledge. Because of that, he received considerable attention. At least I did not have to go out begging for help for my baby boy.

An emotional and significant moment for Scotty and me occurred at three weeks. As he was sound asleep, I held a squeaky toy by his good left ear. I gave a firm squeeze and was sure I saw his eyelids flutter in response. So you bet, I did it again…and again his eyelids fluttered. Once more, and I was pretty sure we had an answer. Yes, he had some level of hearing.

Scotty's Early Years

With all of Scotty's issues and limited funds, I had to stop working toward my degree. I would not trade my journey with Scotty for a degree. My time and effort now had to be dedicated to him. I was able to have a successful career for myself in the real estate title industry as an abstractor and real estate title examiner. I earned enough to give us a living. Even though I was the sole provider for Scotty, he never went without. He always had good clothes, shoes, food, and most importantly, all of his medical needs were met.

To get him the care he needed, I knew I had to research specialists and programs to assist families with handicapped infants. What I needed most urgently was help in feeding my new baby. I was directed to Women, Infants, and Children (WIC). It is a federal supplemental nutritional program for low-income mothers with children under age five. Through WIC, I had fewer worries about feeding my newborn.

As good as the WIC program was, it was not easy to conform. Most WIC recipients did not work, so the program was geared toward mothers who remained home. I had to work to support myself and Scotty. Well, WIC delivers only in the daytime, and the items need to be signed for. I tried explaining to WIC that I worked during the day and Scotty was in day care. It made no difference. Somebody needed to sign, or nothing was delivered. I had to arrange for a friend's husband, who worked nights, to sign and receive my supplies during the day while I was at work.

Next came medical help for Scotty. I learned about the Bureau for Children with Medical Handicaps program of the State of Ohio (BCMH). It is a helpful program linking those with special medical needs with appropriate providers and specialists, including helping with the cost. It is comforting to know there are agencies and organizations dedicated to helping those in desperate need of an advocate.

Mothers needing assistance must learn that help does not come knocking on your door. I have considerable sympathy for all single mothers who may require welfare assistance of some kind. However, one needs to persevere, research, and seek help. It is amazing what is available to help the average person. If one does not work to provide a solid foundation for a child, the cycle of welfare will continue. I did not want a welfare life for Scotty.

Our first couple of years were filled with appointments. Some medical help was available locally, but I was prepared to utilize any specialist who could help. Locally, we sought out any doctor with an appropriate specialty at the Medical College of Ohio (MCO). None with the specialty level Scotty needed for facial issues was available at the time at MCO. A doctor with the right credentials who practiced in Farmington Hills, Michigan, was recommended. With what I discovered about his reputation, I was confident he could help Scotty. Unfortunately, my limited insurance would not cover this doctor. Neither would BCMH since we needed to stay in Ohio for whatever care was needed. That meant going to the Cleveland Clinic for any attention the Medical College of Ohio could not provide.

We visited MCO for our initial meeting with an ENT doctor. Although he had a good reputation, I could tell it was not going to be a comfortable relationship. I asked about getting his tongue clipped. A restricted tongue might contribute to a speech impediment. His minimal hearing alone could affect his pronunciation. The doctor declined to do it and disagreed it needed to be done at all. I was seriously uncomfortable with his inflexibility. I had noticed in Scotty's file that his ear issues were listed incorrectly. They confused his left and right ear status. I pointed out the mistake and was assured they would correct the file. On a subsequent visit, I discovered they had failed to make the change. Enough for me. I wanted someone I was comfortable with.

At the time, I was working with a Wood County advocate for the hearing impaired. When she listened to my situation, she referred me to Dr. Larry Winegar, a Toledo ENT doctor, who had worked with BCMH patients. He was marvelous, and I could tell he was deeply interested in helping Scotty. He agreed it would help to have his tongue clipped.

Scotty was only two at this time. The tongue clipping was an outpatient procedure and the first of many surgeries. I can still picture him in his little hospital gown sitting in bed. He was mesmerized with his tongue: sticking it in and out to try to see it.

Dr. Winegar fitted him for his first hearing aid. It required a special ear mold for his abnormal ear formation. It was a behind-the-ear receiver, without the benefit of much of a "behind" to hang it on. Given the lack of good ear support and the fact he was a little boy, I had to pin the aid to his shirt with a sturdy string. In addition, sometimes I needed to use medical tape to keep the aid in place. Many times during his early years, I discovered the hearing aid dangling from his shirt. He adjusted to it quite well. As he got older, he clearly understood how it worked. I discovered him turning the aid volume down or off whenever I was scolding or nagging him about something.

Once he began wearing a hearing aid regularly, we began seeing Joyce Kinker-Johnson, a credentialed audiologist. She thought the world of Scotty. They even shared the same birthday. She made his molds from then on. He remained in her hearing aid care from the age of two through fifteen. We had begun speech and physical therapy at MCO, so we did not have a lot of free time.

With all of Scotty's struggles, a new problem surfaced. He developed an eye infection in his left eye. It was persistent and kept recurring. It was finally diagnosed as a form of pinkeye, requiring treatment at MCO. He had to have steroid drops administered at the hospital daily for thirty days and wear an eye patch. We even had to go on Easter Sunday. They determined through this treatment that Scotty did not feel pain in that eye.

He evidently had scratched the eye and had felt no discomfort. The ulcer that formed needed to be corrected. Now the treatment was to operate on the eye and sew the eyelid shut until it healed. The eye issues did not keep him from being 100 percent boy. He played rough. Soon after the surgery, he took a swan dive off his bed, landing on his face, suffering a rug burn. This was followed several days later with a fall out of bed, resulting in a black eye to his right eye. His appearance was absolutely horrible. His left eye was sewn shut, with facial rug burns and a black eye. I felt so bad for him. I have to tell you, though, my main concern was that someone might turn me in, assuming child abuse. It was clear when we were out in public; there were skeptical sideways peeks at both of us.

The next several years were full of visits to monitor his development. During this time, we were in survival mode, without much money left after rent and day care. My ex and I had separated, and he was erratic with child support at best or outright declined to pay. Whatever it took to succeed, it would be me persevering on my own, with whatever help my family and God could contribute. Nothing interrupted his development into "Scooter," All-American Boy.

His syndrome had many side issues we needed to overcome. His teeth were of a concern, partly because of how the syndrome affected his mouth structure. And partly of him being Scotty. His front five baby teeth died and turned gray after a playground accident. He attempted one of his ninja dives, landing hard on his face with a mouth full of dirt. In dealing with these dead teeth, they discovered he was missing a saliva gland. Many of his teeth were not benefiting from continuous saliva rinse. Trips to the pediatric dentist affected both of us. He would scream and cry, "Not the Red Chair!" It was the cavity-filling, teeth-pulling chair. On more than one occasion, he would have a tooth extracted, and I would take him to school with gauze to control the bleeding and a can of Spaghettios for lunch. I had no other choice: I had to get to work.

My vacation days were filled with doctor and surgery appointments. Without dental insurance and with BCMH covering only a portion of the cost, I ran a tab. I would pay $10 a month, $20–$50 when I received a quarterly bonus, and the refund from federal tax return. When I finally paid off the debt, the ladies in the dentist office sent me a nice card acknowledging my determination. There were times when both the dentist and the orthodontist waived charges. To this day, I am humbled by the help given to me.

One year, I got ahead of all bills and medical costs by $750. I decided I was not going to do the responsible thing by putting it away for a rainy day. Rather, I would splurge on my son with a vacation. I used the entire amount and took my seven-year-old boy to Cincinnati's Kings Island for two days and the zoo for a third day. Scotty and I went on every big ride he was permitted to ride. None of the gentle rides for Scotty. He still loves roller coasters.

On our way to the zoo, I got lost in a questionable area of Cincinnati. No GPS in those days. I had to rely on a map and ended up asking a public transit bus driver for directions. I was stressed and uneasy, with Scotty totally oblivious to our predicament. Instead, he had his new cassette tape he got from Kings Island blaring the theme song to *The Flintstones*. I am near panic, and here he was bopping along to the music, ignoring the burned-out houses and shabby scenery. We made it to the zoo where he enjoyed every moment.

Litany of Surgeries

In 1993, the serious and more discomforting surgeries began. An attempt was made at the Cleveland Clinic to improve his right jawline by performing a bone graft. It was the first of many inpatient procedures. In less than a month, the graft had to be removed due to an infection. What followed was the most uncomfortable course of treatment I had ever been asked to do. Even more so than giving birth.

The surgical wound would need to heal from the inside out—which meant the incision would have to remain open. I was told to periodically swab and cleanse the wound. The pain to Scotty was horrific. Would I have the courage or composure to continue to inflict such pain to my little boy? Since the wound needed cleaning, I would just have to manage.

About a year later, a second attempt was made at the graft, which was successful. It was an inpatient surgery, which now is beginning to trigger reluctance on Scotty's part.

In 1995, Dr. Winegar determined Scotty would have to undergo sinus surgery to alleviate an ongoing problem. At least this surgery was in a local hospital and not as traumatic. Still, Scotty was beginning to protest any procedure requiring a hospital stay.

While these surgeries addressed his most pressing conditions, his spine began to show signs of small distortion. Dr. E. O. Kelley had been our entire family's dentist for twenty years. As he witnessed the efforts to solve all of Scotty's issues, he became more involved with helping obtain treatment options for his spine. He was a member of the Toledo chapter of Shriners International. Dr. Kelley got the Shriners involved and arranged for the organization to include us in their trips to Chicago to be seen by their spinal surgeon at the Children's Hospital. Surely, Dr. Kelley was an answer to our prayers.

What a truly marvelous organization. They made regular runs to Chicago transporting individuals and family members at no cost. Their courteous, caring drivers would get us there, wait for the appointment to conclude, then drive us back home. We were getting the best spinal care available at no cost and arranged as conveniently as possible. We made these visits concurrently with his other ongoing surgeries and doctor visits.

After careful evaluation, the staff physicians in Chicago wanted to initially try a full torso back brace to encourage a straight normal spine growth. This evaluation went on for two years. During this period, he tried to do all normal boy things, which required removing the brace for the activity, replacing the brace when he was finished. It allowed him to still swim and play Little League baseball among other physical activities.

January 1996, a bone graft to his right ear was attempted at the Cleveland Clinic, with the piece of bone coming from one of his ribs. This was a preliminary procedure to prepare him for ear reconstruction. Our doctor at the clinic was a capable person, but this was to be a new attempt for him. I simply could not afford to travel, stay at a distant facility, and incur the cost of the surgery in order to have the best available surgeons for ear reconstruction. The clinic doctor was our only hope.

Several months later, in 1996, we returned to Cleveland for a reconstruction surgery on his right ear, followed a month later with a skin graft. Both were inpatient procedures, which was difficult to explain to Scotty. Things were now coming at us fast, with barely enough healing time between surgeries before the next surgery was scheduled. Too bad, E-ZPasses were not yet available on the Ohio Turnpike.

"Time for My Solo"

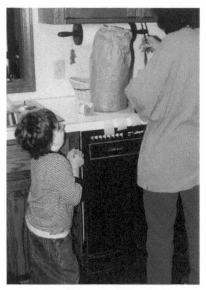

*"Mom, can't we skip cleaning
the wound today, please"*

"Put Me in Coach"

"It only hurts when I smile"

Too cute not to include

I LOVE MY MOM & DAD

Into Our Life Comes a Rescuer

I was getting weary traveling this journey as a solo parent. A single mom with Scotty's issues does not have many opportunities or time for a relationship. Oh, someone may be interested in a short-term relationship, but a longer commitment including a handicapped child was not going to happen. I had already witnessed too many single women settle for brief affairs providing them with some diversion, with no benefit to their children or happiness. I was not going to be that kind of mother.

It was during this span of surgeries I met John. He was different, seemed sincere, a good Christian, and was seeking the same thing as I was: a good family life. There was mutual attraction. Yes, I was attracted to John, and he to me. That's not the mutual attraction I mean. It was the attraction between Scotty and John. Genuine affection developed between those two.

I first met John at the annual Polish Festival in Toledo. We had a pleasant exchange, but I did not encourage anything further. A year later, a friend and I went to a coworker's family cottage in the Irish Hills where our paths crossed again. I was lying on a raft on the lake when I saw John and his good friend coming down the hill to the cottage. He had on a Hawaiian shirt, as I recall. I quickly recognized it was the guy with whom I had an enjoyable conversation the year before.

Quite a group gathered by late afternoon. Someone said they were in the mood for a frozen cocktail. We concurred it would be refreshing. I saw John quietly leave. He returned about forty-five minutes later with a blender, ice, and all the fixings for daiquiris. I had to laugh at his spontaneity. He was an entertaining, funny guy.

We went for a boat ride, and I got to watch John water ski. Hmm, funny and athletic. In the evening, we had a bonfire, and John and I sat next to each other. We talked and talked long into the night. John made me laugh. Mutual attraction was evident, so I told him, "You know…I'm a package deal." I went on to explain my life with Scotty. He did not seem fazed by the revelation I was a mom. Not an ordinary mom, but one with a special needs child.

We exchanged phone numbers this time to be sure that we could reconnect.

Gosh, I was giddy when I returned home. I told Mom and a close friend about this new guy. He called the following Tuesday and asked me to be his date for a family wedding the following Saturday. Although I had a blind date the Friday before, I was indeed free for Saturday. The Friday date came for me in a fancy sports car. He turned out to be a pretty pretentious and arrogant jerk. The date was over before we made it up the hill of my apartment complex parking lot.

Why is this blind date relevant? The next night, John arrived in his well-worn Pontiac LeMans Hatchback. I got into the passenger side, and he told me I need to straddle the floorboard because of a hole. The backseat was full of clutter, including an old pizza box with leftovers from who knows when. Okay, here we go, our first date was a family wedding. We laughed because he told me later, "I had to see if I liked you before I spent any real money on you." My response has always been, "What a cheap guy, taking me out for a free dinner for our first date." I always thought it amusing I fell in love with the cheap guy with a crap car over one with a Corvette.

That family wedding, actually, helped contribute to our relationship. I met his entire family: both sides. They were a truly enjoyable, caring group of people. I was immediately comfortable and felt blessed. John's gift to the newlyweds was a clue that John may be even more frugal than a cheap first date. The gift was the blender he had purchased at the cottage party, cleaned and wrapped nicely. Next came some private time with John's parents. For this step in our relationship, I believed Scotty should be with us. Scotty took to them easily, and John's parents, Barb and Jerry Noonan, were affectionate in return.

We dated from August 1993 until John proposed on November 18, 1995. During our two years together, he was working full-time at Overnight Transportation and at Old Dominion Transportation. He had completed his college degree in criminal justice and had been attempting to secure a position in law enforcement. He was intent on landing a position in a good-sized city police department or as a

U.S. Marshal. It was a slow period for such hires. I believe John felt he needed a good career position in order to get serious about me.

All the while, John's family fully accepted Scotty. They were all so fond of him that he was being treated just like family. John's younger brother, Jeff, was in college at Cincinnati at the time. He actually brought Scotty down for "Little Sibs" Weekend and all the activities that were involved. His mother, Barb, took Scotty to Nashville to spend time with John's sister, Bonnie. He was slowly being embraced by a new family.

What I did not know until later was how John's wise mother, Barb, had counseled John. One day when Scotty and I were with John and his folks, Scotty ran across the floor and hopped up on the couch to sit close to Jerry. They got into a typical Scotty-to-adult conversation. Barb pulled John aside to have a private conversation. She had noted how Scotty was getting attached to John and to the two of them. She told John to think about his relationship with me, and if it was not going to go further, he should end it soon. Barb stressed to John that Scotty already had a challenging life, and he did not deserve to be disappointed over losing people in his life with whom he was becoming attached.

John was readily accepted by my family. Clearly they felt a sense of relief to have someone special in my life. When little things needed a man's attention with my car or apartment, Dad filled that void. I don't believe it bothered him to be called upon for the occasional mouse or repair problem, but when John entered the picture, I had a feeling Dad welcomed the help. Scotty being a rough little boy caused his share of broken things. One repair job I asked Dad about was a hole Scotty punched in the drywall caused by banging his bedroom door open. When I showed it to Dad, he said he would see what he could do. Shortly after that, John saw the hole and fixed it. When Dad saw John's professional looking repair job, he said, "Find a way to keep him around." Whether he approved of John yet became irrelevant. It was clear John's help in taking care of Scotty and me had Dad's approval.

John kept applying and searching for his opportunity. It was only a matter of time. He received offers from the Toledo Police Department (TPD) and from the Columbus Police Department. As he was reviewing the offers, we talked about our situation. He had a real interest in the Columbus opportunity. As much as it made me uncomfortable, I told John, with no ring on my finger, he needed to know I would not uproot Scotty from his school, his doctors, or my family support group.

He selected the TPD position. He knew he could not remove us from my family and all the medical support we had developed in the Toledo area. After he successfully went through the background checks and physical, he knew he had secured a position. Next would be the police academy. He was confident he would do well in the training program, so he went out and bought an engagement ring.

During our engagement, he always included Scotty. Once when I was leaving for work and taking Scotty to school, I found a bouquet of six roses outside my apartment door, along with a box of Teenage Mutant Ninja Turtle fruit snacks and a balloon for Scooter. He fell in love with Scotty before me. I knew I had the right guy for both of us.

Our Wedding

My first marriage was a simple civil ceremony. John had never been married. We wanted a nice formal wedding that our families agreed to. John and I had worked closely with Father Joe Steinbauer of All Saints Catholic Church in Rossford. We wanted a full Catholic wedding and needed Father Joe to assist in making that happen. He was marvelous, understanding, and helpful. John had a close cousin studying for the priesthood. Jim Halleron had progressed to deacon at the time and could not celebrate the wedding Mass, but he was able to perform the marriage portion. Father Joe celebrated the mass.

The wedding was every bit as important to Scotty as to me. Since he was a capable young boy, we believed Scotty should play a prominent role. He was fitted with his own little tux. There were several key roles for him. His initial role was to escort my mom to her seat. Next came the important role of escorting me to the altar along with my father. During the mass, we entrusted him with reading the petitions. Imagine a little ten-year-old on a stool to reach the microphone, addressing a church full of people. That's my Scotty.

My parents said they witnessed a number of hankies dabbing tears. It was a truly joyous occasion.

After the wedding reception, Scotty and John had a private moment. As he was sitting on John's lap, he asked, "Now can I call you Dad?" We decided to forego a honeymoon and instead took Scotty to Disney World that summer. My dream honeymoon to the Caribbean would have to wait. We made this wedding vacation all about Scotty. We went sailing with the captain, letting Scotty take the helm. Scotty got his chance to go deep-sea fishing, thanks to John's effort to make the trip memorable.

John Adopts Scotty

For some time, John and I wanted Scotty to be officially adopted by John. His last name would be the same as our family name, Noonan. A good Irish name. Scotty's biological father was reluctant to agree, even though he had not been in Scotty's life for quite some time. When we had our first child together, John and I became more aggressive in seeking approval for adoption. Adoption when the biological father is hesitant to sign off is a difficult and time-consuming legal process.

We were determined to make it happen. In 2000, with the help of an attorney, we initiated the adoption process. In Lucas County, Ohio, the probate court has jurisdiction over adoptions. Judge Jack Puffenberger, the presiding judge, was responsible for shepherding our adoption request through the system. It took a year until all the legal issues were resolved and the path to adoption was clear. Judge Puffenberger was exceptionally sympathetic and helpful in resolving the matter. He made it a grand ceremony in his courtroom attended by all our family. Now we were all Noonans. Scotty's first question, once his name was officially Noonan, was, "Am I Irish now?"

This was such an important event in our life that we celebrated by renting a hall and throwing a huge party. Our families were all included, as well as numerous friends. John and Scotty wore white golf shirts embroidered with a shamrock with "Noonan" lettering. Our two-and-a-half-year-old Blake had his own shamrock shirt with "I'm a Noonan too!" on it.

Father Joe and Scotty
First Communion

A Family at last

Scotty lands a big one

Officially a Noonan
L–R: Fr. Halleron; Judge Puffenberger; John Donahue, attorney; Lois
& Bob Johnson, friends; John; My Mom; Scott; Barb; Jerry; ME; My
Dad; Kyle; Blake; Cynthia; Corey; Casey; Uncle "Larry"; "Miss Nancy".
Photo taken by Cynthia's husband, Joe. Kathy the lizard not pictured.

Judge Puffenberger swearing in Scott for
Board of Developmental Disabilities

Our New Life Goes On

January 1997 found us back in the Cleveland Clinic for another procedure for Scotty's right ear. Our whole family made a trip to Our Lady of Consolation National Shrine to pray for this surgery. This was followed in *August 1997*, with a second sinus surgery in Toledo. Due to his facial issues, he suffered from repeated sinus infections, and the second surgery would help correct the problem. These were both inpatient surgeries. Compared to what was coming next, these surgeries were minor annoyances. Next would come the most traumatic and riskiest surgery Scotty would experience.

After a lengthy evaluation period filled with follow-up appointments in Chicago and numerous X-rays, the course of treatment for his spine was recommended. The back brace was providing only nominal benefit. Indications were his spine would distort significantly as he continued to grow. It was decided that he should have a posterior and anterior spinal fusion. A steel rod in front of the spine and a second one along the back would work to keep scoliosis at bay. The choice was not easy. They could do the process in stages—an initial fusion now, followed by another fusion with steel rods four years later. Waiting four years for the second stage would permit close-to-normal physical growth. Done at only one surgical session would mean his overall height would be compromised and head and neck movement restricted.

Because the surgery was traumatic and risky, we opted for one and done sacrificing his overall height. I am sure he would like those extra inches now. At the time, it seemed best. The surgeon wanted to get started as soon as possible.

Spinal Fusion Surgery

So in *October 1997*, we made the trip to Chicago and the Shriners Children's Hospital. John, my now new husband of six months, drove us there and stayed with us. The Children's Hospital was in a semi residential neighborhood. Upon getting close to the hospital, we could detect the sweet smell of the M&M factory next door.

My parents came over the morning of the actual surgery. I needed their prayers to go along with John's supporting hugs. Leaving nothing to chance, though, we were blessed with Father Jim Halleron's arrival from Mansfield, Ohio, just before surgery. We were hopeful with Father Jim present, all our prayers might carry a little more *punch*. I was able to spend some comforting moments in private with Father Jim to help me process all my fears and emotions. I then went off by myself to pray to the Blessed Virgin Mary. I have prayed before, but never this focused. I suppose I prayed like many people, with my mind frequently wandering as I would lose concentration. Now I would not be distracted. I had a clear and crucial request for Mary: "Please keep my boy safe and guide the hands of our surgeon." I believe one mother was comforting another.

We felt so blessed to have a truly gifted, caring surgeon, Dr. Peter Smith, leading the operation. He had been evaluating Scotty since age three. At this writing, he is still helping young children at the Shriner's Hospital. The surgical plan was to do the two spinal fusions a week apart. The time estimate would be six to seven hours each time.

The time had come for Scotty to be prepped for surgery. He had been nervous and quiet to this point. My tough and resilient little guy seemed to melt away. Once he was taken into the prep area, he slowly began to yield to the enormity he was facing. At ten, he was old enough to understand just how difficult this surgery and recovery would be.

Looking around the prep area was like watching something simulated for a T.V. audience. Soft music was playing and a bright yellow glow from the lighting illuminated the whole area. The room had its own distinct clean, antiseptic smell. The operating staff was a flurry of activity, each with a responsibility they fulfilled with an impressive efficiency. Two nurses began working with Scotty. Once on the gurney, he became increasingly agitated. He was in a seated position as he was being hooked up to monitors and IV ports inserted. His head was glancing left then right as he tried to follow every movement of the nurses while expressing his displeasure and apprehension. I could hardly watch as the medical staff persisted over his objections and fear. His tears and resistance were absolutely heartbreaking. John, though, was strong and attended to Scotty, soothing and reassuring him, all the while helping to restrain him.

It was a pitiful sight as they wheeled him into the operating room. What have I allowed? Once he was under and the surgery started, we would get our first report. After an hour or so passed, we became a little concerned. From what we had learned through previous surgeries, Scotty has a difficult anatomy for *intubation,* the insertion of a breathing tube when anesthetizing a surgical patient. For the anesthetist, it can be tedious and time-consuming to get the patient ready. When we received the first report, they explained they had a difficult time with the intubation. The anesthesiologist had even referred to a textbook.

Hour after hour passed with little information. It was getting late in the day. I worried about how his little body could withstand the trauma. Finally, Dr. Smith came in with his progress report. It had gone well, and he was pleased. He paused and offered his assessment. He wanted to continue and do the second surgery. Scotty was doing well, and they wanted to proceed, given how difficult it would be to anesthetize him again.

The surgeon wanted our permission to continue. My dad quickly asked Dr. Smith if he believed he had the stamina to go another five hours. Continuing would make it a twelve-hour surgery. He reassured us he was fine; plus, he knew he had a good team. The team believed it was the best thing to do for Scotty. We had been under Dr. Smith's care long enough to know he was special. We had such confidence in him and his whole staff of caring people at the Shriners Hospital. So we gave the green light.

Post-Operation Recovery

If I believed it was pitiful to watch him wheeled into the operating room, it was minor to what greeted me in recovery. He was kept in ICU, heavily sedated for his comfort and the pain. He was in a nearly comatose state for several days. I stayed by his bedside the entire time. In the ICU, it was unsettling seeing him hooked to machines and having a respiratory therapist come in every few hours for treatments. Scotty was engulfed with tubes and wires and encased in a body brace.

After three days, we were informed that he likely could hear us. We were requested to offer encouraging words. My mom took his little hand and told him she loved him and we would stay by his side. She asked him if he could hear her and to squeeze her hand if he could. She was thrilled to feel a gentle squeeze.

We spent long periods in shifts staying with him and talking to him. Being an avid Cleveland Indians fan, his first words coming out of the anesthetic and sedation were to ask who had won last night's game. The Indians were in the American League playoffs against the New York Yankees when he went into surgery. He had missed the results not only of that game, but that Cleveland had also won the series. Dr. Smith was a Yankee fan. He kept Scotty engaged by razzing him.

The hospital stay lasted three weeks. I stayed for the entire period. John returned to Toledo for his four-day shifts and returned on his days off. He had a cousin in the Chicago area with whom he was able to stay. I was with Scotty all day every day except once. My mom and dad stayed with him while John took me to dinner in a nice restaurant in Chicago: *a pizza parlor!*

I had been given two tickets to game 5 of the World Series with the Marlins in Cleveland. Scotty, adamantly, said he could handle the drive and sitting in the stands and wanted to go. Only weeks after his back surgery, no way were we attempting something so foolish. I gave the tickets to friends.

We returned to Toledo in time for Scotty to watch the final World Series game against the Marlins. Once home, we were able to catch game 7 from the comfort of our own couch only to watch them be one out away from winning and lose. "Damn Jose Mesa" is a phrase we use to this day. The 1997 World Series was a godsend. It was a great distraction for us both.

By the time Scotty came home from the hospital, he had already missed a month of school. He would continue his recuperation through the rest of the calendar year, over Christmas and into the New Year, before being able to return to school. We made a number of follow-up visits to Chicago to assess his recovery. He would live in a torso brace for six months.

Physical Limitations

Even with this back surgery, Scotty was only temporarily side-lined from all the sports he enjoyed, except football. Definitely, football was out. The steel rods in his back would limit him, and the risk would be too great. After full recuperation, he was back to being all-boy. He was able to play Little League baseball, basketball, and soccer for several more years until the effort became too great for his limitations. It was not his first attempt at baseball.

Years previously, when he was seven, I registered him for Rossford Little League. The whole family was furnished with his schedule, and usually turned out for his games. We were fortunate to be assigned a good person as his coach. By good, I mean a man who made sure all the boys got to play, and who was not obsessed with winning at this age. He was good to Scotty and made sure he got as much playing time as all the boys on the team. Scotty wanted to play: winning was a vague concept to him.

When it was his time to bat, he brought smiles to our faces. His antics at the plate were pure entertainment. He had watched enough baseball to know how the skilled batters prepared themselves and what rituals they performed at bat. He imitated the best. He would pound and pound the plate repeatedly to announce he was ready. He got giggles and laughter as he whacked away at the poor home plate.

It was never clear how well he was seeing the ball being tossed to him by an adult coach. He connected often enough to make it interesting. Usually, little rollers in the infield or a blooper barely clearing the pitcher. If he managed to get to first safely, it was as if he had hit a grand-slam home run to win the game. Hands were thrust into the air in the style of "Rocky Balboa," complete with a victory dance.

As entertaining as he was at bat, it was pure slapstick when he played center field. Two defensive plays we all still talk about brought loud laughter. The first was a ball that got through the infield and rolled out to left center field. Scotty and the left fielder raced for the ball and got to it simultaneously. There was a lengthy tug-of-war and some wrestling to control the ball. The two boys were too engaged to react appropriately. In the meantime, the other team's players were circling the bases.

The second instance was equally delightful. On a ball hit to short center field, Scotty fielded it easily. He made a wild wind-up motion, spun around, and released the ball as hard as he could manage. It was a high throw that would have easily made it to the second baseman, except he had stopped his spin facing left field. The ball sailed over the left fielder's head deep into left field. He had no idea where the ball had gone since he fell to the ground after the throw. Once again, the opponents circled the bases.

At this age, Scotty was in constant motion and eager to try anything. He feared nothing and was not shy about trying something new. This became abundantly clear one summer when our whole family went to SeaWorld, which was over by Cleveland. All in all, an enjoyable day interrupted by small rain showers.

The final activity of the day was to permit Scooter and his two younger cousins, Corey and Kyle, to climb into the massive jungle gym play area containing all sorts of tubes, rope ladders, and bridges with observation areas. It was on multiple levels, which meant the boys could go laterally and vertically. Rain had prevented their being able to play earlier in this jungle of ropes and piping. Later in the day, the weather cleared nicely. We were now ready to leave, but wanted to give the boys an opportunity to explore this attraction. The boys were instructed to stay close to the ground, as we intended to call them down after a brief period. We all tried to keep them in sight. After about fifteen minutes, Corey and Kyle, having been pretty responsible, stayed within sight.

Scooter, on the other hand, managed to get deep into the apparatus and several levels up. With him, it was never clear: *Did he not hear? Did he not understand? Or did he not care?* I never seemed comfortable in disciplining him, knowing he may not be totally aware as to why he was being disciplined. Not that he worried about it. It was time to get going for the long drive home, and he was nowhere in sight. We all circled the structure, calling his name, all his names. *Did he not hear, did he not understand, or did he not care?* To the family's amusement, I had to crawl into this play area hunched over and hunt for him. Greg, aka Uncle Larry, crawled in to help me. With two of us chasing him down, we thought we had an even chance. Greg was much taller and had the bigger challenge in hunkering down to maneuver through the maze designed for small children. Those on the ground tried to give some help by pointing out his location, all the while laughing. We eventually trapped him and escorted him down.

Scotty's Final Surgeries

We had a two-year break from surgeries and hospital stays. Scotty had numerous follow-up and evaluation appointments for ongoing issues. These were simply inconveniences in our lives. We returned to the Cleveland Clinic on *August 30, 1999*, for Scotty's next surgery: a jaw distraction device was inserted. Inpatient again. It was a step forward that had to be reversed within two weeks. The distraction device was defective and had to be removed in an emergency surgery. The second device worked fine and was removed in *November 1999*. It meant another night as an inpatient. The device protruded through his lower cheek, permitting me to slowly extend the jawline.

We recognized we were getting close to resolving as many issues as we could. One facial issue remained: a complicated one. In *June 2003*, he had a cheekbone and chin reconstruction to provide better facial symmetry. It required bone grafts. The bone was taken from his skull. Again, two incisions. Scotty received minimal benefit from this surgery and declined to undergo any more efforts to alter his appearance.

Hearing Improvement

Scotty continued to struggle with hearing. A new hearing aid method first developed in Europe in 1977 became commercially available in 1987. It involved inserting a titanium rod directly into the skull behind an ear. An instrument is snapped onto this rod. This hearing method is called bone anchored hearing aid (BAHA). It is designed to transfer sound through bone conduction, greatly improving clarity and volume. The anchored hearing aid converts sound to vibrations, which are sent through the skull bone directly to the inner ear.

Assistance through the Bureau for Children with Medical Handicaps was coming to a close soon due to Scotty's adoption by John. Dr. Winegar had continued to give Scotty excellent care and was still aggressively working to help us. He recommended we consider this BAHA device. It was especially effective for hearing issues such as Scotty's. However, when Scott learned that another surgery and another hospital stay would be required, he strongly protested. Dr. Winegar wisely demonstrated how the device worked by affixing a BAHA headband.

Scotty immediately heard new sounds. "Where are those voices coming from?" Dr. Winegar said they were people talking in the next examining room. We were given the unit to take home to give Scotty more opportunity to experience the benefit. A number of new sounds startled Scott. He heard a humming noise in our kitchen for the first time: our refrigerator. In our backyard, he heard scratching, scraping noises: a squirrel scampering up a tree. Hearing these new sounds changed Scott's mind, and he could not wait to get this new device. He was one of the first in northwest Ohio to receive a BAHA. Scotty insisted in being awake for the installation. It was a delicate process with infection or rejection not uncommon. Scotty adapted well, and after an infection at the post site, he learned how to better care for that area. To this day, though, he has declined to undergo surgery for a new improved version or to obtain one for his other ear. His relationship with Dr. Winegar was so strong that Dr. Winegar sent him a gift when he graduated from high school.

After seventeen years of oral surgeries, oral braces, back braces, reconstructive surgeries, and eye patches, speech therapy, and physical therapy, Scotty was done. Not because no issues remained, but because he had had enough. He accepted himself as he was and believed others would too.

Scotty's Pets

As Scotty was going through all this trauma, I wanted to do something special for him. A pet seemed to be a way to reward him for his tolerance and toughness. Aunt Nancy, aka Miss Nancy, bought him a hamster for his fifth birthday. The hamster did not do well and soon appeared to be suffering. I tried to save the little thing by frantically rushing out to locate some gerbil/hamster medicine. No luck, it died.

For his seventh birthday, I bought him a lizard. Don't ask me why. I believed he needed something unusual to keep his attention. I had been dating John for several months and stored the lizard at his parents for a few days until Scotty's party. The lizard did not create much interest. All it did for hours was cling to a branch in its terrarium. One thing I had not considered is having to make regular stops at a pet store to purchase live crickets.

Scotty thought he needed to have a name for his lizard. After tossing out several names, his choice was "Kathy." I had no clue where he got that name. He did not even know a Kathy. I did not know he even knew the name Kathy. It was so like him. I told him the name did not fit a lizard. He insisted it was his choice. I kept debating the name and employed some strategy. I told him the lizard seemed to be a male and a female name was not right. So a lizard named Kathy became a lizard named Rocky. The name did not matter, given its short life.

It was disgusting to watch Rocky eat. However, it at least made some movement. Rocky was usually stationary. We watched it for a while one day after dropping in a live cricket. It did not chase after the cricket. We assumed it was not hungry yet. We checked on it periodically, and it sat immobile clinging to a small branch. After several days, I dropped in another live cricket since it surely should have been hungry. It was immobile because it was dead. Rocky was followed some time later by a gerbil. It turned out I had no "green thumb" when it came to small pets. The gerbil died shortly after moving to our new house in South Toledo.

John's job as a police officer for Toledo required him to live within the city. I had promised Scotty a dog if we ever lived in a house with a nice yard. Without informing me, John took Scotty out to buy a puppy. So typical of John with Scotty. Scotty loved this dog and named her Misty. This time there was no name debate. He named her Misty, end of discussion. He now had something of his own to show him affection and unconditional love. He had earned it.

We had Misty for nine years until she developed cancer behind an eye. At the same time, Joshua, our youngest, had to be hospitalized with asthma. It became clear his asthma was at least partly due to Misty's dog dander. The cancer was going to claim Misty sooner than later, so we had no choice: we could not keep her. It was difficult for Scotty. Years later, I found Misty's dog collar among his mementos.

Scotty's Education

During all this surgery activity and visits to the Cleveland Clinic, Scotty was trying to get an education. I believe Scotty's education began with his time in day care. At six weeks, he was enrolled in Mercy Hospital's day care. How reassuring it was when I learned that the head of day care was my eighth-grade teacher at St. Rose Parochial School. It took away some apprehension when I entrusted Scotty with someone who I knew and respected.

I was not happy having to put him in day care at six weeks of age. I was the sole provider at the time, and did not intend to raise my child on welfare. I believed I was better than that. I wanted Scotty to know from the beginning, I would do whatever it took to provide for him. I worked downtown not far from Mercy Hospital which made me even more at ease. When I would get him after work, the route we would take to get on the expressway went through an interesting part of Toledo.

When Scotty grew older, he enjoyed gawking around as I drove us home. On the way to the expressway entrance, due to turns and traffic signal timing, we would always catch a red light at the same intersection. This intersection was a prime spot for ladies of the evening, escorts, working girls, if you follow. At this age, he was "Scooter." He loved people and would engage anyone. So he would smile and wave to his friends, the "pretty ladies," as he called them. And God bless them, they would smile and wave back. For some, it may have been the only genuine affectionate smile they would see that day.

We moved to Rossford where he attended two different day cares. Scotty was treated like any other child and was well liked. He was able to go on various field trips during the summer months, which added greatly to his development. By now, it was only us, so I made time each evening for a lesson. I would teach him colors, letters, numbers, animals, etc. Still unsure of his eyesight or hearing, I would put the object, letter, color, or number flashcard against my cheek. With him focused on my lips after seeing the card, I would state the object's name and its sound—loudly! For animals, I would have him repeat the sound made by the animal along with its identity. We would do this exercise most weekday evenings for a while or for as long as I had his attention.

We were still renting an apartment in Rossford when he began kindergarten. Given his issues, he had to be evaluated by the district's school psychologist. After a two-hour assessment period, he believed he knew enough about Scotty to make a recommendation. Scotty was five at the time and had been doing one hundred piece puzzles for the past year. He was a normal boy for his age playing Nintendo and obsessed with Teenage Mutant Ninja Turtles and Power Rangers.

The psychologist's assessment was troubling. He believed it would be best for Scotty to be enrolled into the Toledo public school system: specifically at Oakdale Elementary School five miles away in East Toledo. The school had classes for children with special needs: more specifically autistic children. From my personal experience working with Scotty, I believed he was ready for a regular school. Although he was the expert, the psychologist's assessment failed Scotty miserably. I have always believed he was trying to avoid Rossford having to make any accommodation. It was business rather than what would be best for Scotty. He explained how beneficial it would be for Scotty's development. As he was continuing to talk, I was shaking my head no—just no!

I was adamant Scotty should be allowed to attend kindergarten at Indian Hills elementary, the school to which he normally would be assigned. I was granted a meeting with Mrs. Smith, the pre-k and kindergarten teacher, Mrs. Wonstetler, the principal, and the school psychologist. I truly believed Scotty needed the exposure and socialization school could provide. I pleaded for consideration for some alternative permitting Scotty to be mainstreamed.

Ignoring the psychologist's protest, Mrs. Smith and Mrs. Wonstetler agreed to have him attend pre-k for the year, after which they would reassess his progress and potential. Not what I had hoped for at the time, however, it was a great opportunity for Scotty to shine. He had Mrs. Smith for pre-k for a half day and then went to day care. They developed an individualized education program (IEP), and I met quarterly with them to review Scotty's progress.

The following year, he went to all-day kindergarten with Mrs. Smith. At the end of this second school year, Mrs. Smith, Principal Wonstetler, and Mrs. Laubenthal, the first-grade teacher, met with me to reassess Scotty's progress. Their decision was an unconventional approach, which forever endeared me to these educators. Scotty was behind in his physical development and, coupled with his weak hearing his first two years, meant he had ground to cover.

The plan was to have Scotty repeat kindergarten in the morning and join the first grade in the afternoon. Rossford schools had arranged for a lavalier-style sending unit for the teachers and a special receiver for Scotty. It made it easier for the teacher to project without worrying whether Scotty could hear well. Even today, when I explain how Scotty was mainstreamed, people are impressed by these educators' courage and ingenuity. The following year, he went to first grade the full year. Mrs. Laubenthal was as amazing as Mrs. Smith. Both had him for two years. With their acceptance and effort, Scotty began to blossom. He was clearly now ready to follow a regular educational schedule. We held him back in order to move him forward.

His first Christmas in school meant his first children's Christmas program for parents and family. He had his own cheering section as our whole family turned out, seizing the center seating. They were counting on being entertained by Scooter, and I am sure, thinking perhaps they could distract him, creating some amusing activity. I had given Scoot some last-minute direction: "No picking your nose, and pay attention." The little children filed in, taking their positions on the risers. Both pleas for good behavior were disregarded within the first thirty seconds onstage. To our benefit, Scooter was close to the end of the first row and nearest to where we were sitting. He was standing with his hands in his little pockets and gawking around at the time.

My sisters noisily gestured and got his attention before the program began. As soon as he caught sight of us, he pulled his hands from his pockets and started running across the stage to join us. Two teachers were quickly responsive and intercepted him before he got to the edge of the stage. I was embarrassed, but the rest of the family got their amusement before the evening's program began.

I tried to provide as many activities I could to aid his development and give him more socialization with children his age. A program offered weekly after school was a session of bowling at a local alley. It was a wonderful two-hour program. A school bus would take the children directly to the bowling alley after school. He loved to bowl. I would come after work, pick him up, and take him to McDonald's for a Happy Meal to further the treat for him. It was another opportunity to add to his experiences and interact with others his age.

We Move to Toledo

As much as he benefitted from beginning his schooling in Rossford, we were unable to continue. We had to move to Toledo. As a Toledo police officer, John was required to live within the city's boundary. We found a nice home in the South Toledo's Beverly area. It was a nice tree-lined area with a park one block down and a block over. We had been in our home for several days when Scotty asked to go to the park. At ten, he was old enough, and the area safe enough even though he would be out of sight. He was gone longer than we would have liked, and I became a little concerned. We were about to set out to search for him when the telephone rang. It was someone who lived one street over calling about Scotty.

Scotty told us he thought it was time to go home, but was uncertain as to what direction to go. After walking around for a short time, he knew he needed help. No problem for resourceful Scotty as he is not intimidated by strangers or a strange situation. He picked a house, strolled to the front door, and rang the doorbell. He greeted the person who answered the door with, "Hi, my name's Scott, and I can't find my way home." Our new neighbor related the story to us. Scotty did not know how to get home. He had explained he was new to the neighborhood and gave her his phone number. No sitting on the curb in tears for my boy.

Our home was within walking distance to an excellent public elementary school and a parochial school. Scotty was entering the third grade. Our intent was to provide a Catholic education to help him expand his religious education. He had been receiving religious education through Confraternity of Christian Doctrine (CCD) program at Rossford All Saints Catholic Church. He was able to make his first communion with Father Joe while attending second grade at Indian Hills Elementary.

We enrolled Scotty at Our Lady of Perpetual Help (OLPH). The school had an excellent reputation, and we were comfortable sending him there. We believed that with his physical issues, it might be a more welcoming environment. I met with the principal and his first teacher requesting he not be given any special treatment, nor should he be coddled. Given his engaging personality and sweet disposition, the good-hearted teachers could not resist doing either.

In the fall, while in the fourth grade, he had his major back surgery, forcing him to miss school until the following calendar year. We received tremendous support from the OLPH family. Mrs. Kathy Dusseau, the school's director of religious education, and his OLPH teachers had given him special attention, so he was able to keep up with the assignments while absent. Some study assignments were provided before he left for surgery.

Mrs. Dusseau put together an extensive photo album for him to have with him as a way to keep him company while away. And the cards, tons of notes, and get-well wishes were constantly coming in from his OLPH family. Scotty developed a special relationship with Mrs. Dusseau, and it continues to this day. Because of all he had overcome, she has had him speak about his experiences and facing adversity to confirmants at OLPH and St. Rose in Perrysburg.

In the eighth grade, Mrs. Dusseau knew Scotty wanted to be Jesus in the Living Stations of the Cross. It was a program staged in the church annually by the eighth grade. She knew he would do well and gave him the part. He did a marvelous job. Even this solemn event gave us pause. Scotty presented a sympathetic Jesus and played his role as seriously as we have ever seen him. It was particularly touching when "Christ fell for the third time." The cross he was carrying brushed Scotty's hearing aid, knocking it to the floor. A centurion character discreetly grabbed it and slipped it to Scotty. Even though a number of students knew what had happened, they never broke character and maintained the dignity of the performance.

Throughout his attendance at OLPH, he was provided a speech therapist, Mr. Arrington, from the Toledo Public Schools. Poor Mr. Arrington. He worked with Scotty, making good progress. Another jaw surgery then would put them back to the beginning. He continued playing Little League baseball for OLPH and expanded into basketball and soccer for the years offered. His participation was interrupted by surgeries. He would have loved to play football. It just was not possible. However, he served as team manager from grade five through grade eight.

As much as he enjoyed sports, his physical limits and absences kept him from developing. He was always given opportunities to participate. He just wanted to play along with his friends. He had no hidden talent for basketball. That actually made it more entertaining. When he tossed the ball inbounds, he was not particularly concerned with whether he stepped over the line before making the inbounds pass. Dribbling and steps were problems for him, making it entertaining. He was not at all sensitive about our laughter.

Clearly soccer could have been his sport. Not the one he preferred, but the one not dependent upon size. He was quick and aggressive getting to the ball. It gave him a chance to tangle with friends and classmates, and his play earned him a degree of respect. What became noticeable, though, was his stamina. He played hard, needing to slow down occasionally. Nothing stopped him for long. He knew by seventh grade, he would not be able to participate in any more sports. The games became too fast and required more flexibility and stamina.

Scotty with Rose Bowl Star
Joe Germaine

Carrying Cross for Jesus

Highschool Graduation Photo

Win one for the Gipper

Senior Day at Central Catholic Football game

Another Side to Scotty

During his years at OLPH, Scotty grew immensely in knowledge and maturity. His personality has been described throughout this story. Another aspect needs to be covered: he was never ever devious or mean. Although some may describe him as a bit mischievous, it was not the case. Perhaps naïve would be a better description. He had this tendency to not foresee the consequences of a decision he might make or what a certain action might lead to. This problem resulted in some uncomfortable situations—all to the amusement of family.

Once, Scotty got home from school to find himself locked out with nobody home. Faced with this dilemma, he gave it some thought. Not enough thought, however, for his plan was to smash in the garage service door window. He could enter the house through the garage. Problem solved.

On another occasion, Scotty and a friend found a lighter while they were behind the Christian School next to OLPH. They began setting little objects on fire. They soon were surprised by a security person. Their reaction was to toss everything into a nearby dumpster and take off. The dumpster caught fire, and authorities began looking for the two involved. The neighborhood around these schools was predominantly white. Scotty had his own unique appearance, and his friend was a mixed-race fellow student at OLPH. No mystery as to the two perpetrators. It was a minor infraction. Scotty's father, John, being a police officer and vouching for the boys, helped prevent any serious action against them.

When he was old enough to be left alone for brief periods, Scotty had specific instructions to stay in the house and no friends. One early evening, John and I went to the store, leaving Scotty alone in his pajamas. No need to restate the rules: he knew what they were. Imagine our surprise as we were driving home on the six-lane major roadway that passed in front of OLPH. There on the grassy landscaped medium strip was a young boy sitting on his bicycle. As we passed, we could tell it was Scotty in his pajamas. I do not believe he grasped why he needed to be disciplined.

Scotty's attendance at OLPH was a life changer. He blossomed in that environment and made lifelong friends with classmates and adults. Even after graduating from the eighth grade, he continued to be involved in parish and school activities, working on their annual Lenten fish fry and parish festival. He chaired the twentieth-anniversary festival.

Next Up, High School

Academically, Scotty was competitive. Upon graduation, scholarships were awarded to attend a Catholic high school, with some designated for specific high schools. At the time, we were considering St. Francis de Sales, an all-boys school, and Toledo Central Catholic, a coed school. Both would offer a good learning environment and a solid education. Either would be expensive for us. We were resolved to find a way to cover the cost.

We toured Central Catholic during an open house for eighth-graders. We were encouraged by what this private religious school could provide Scotty. Plus, it was John's alma mater. During our tour, the head football coach saw Scotty and came over to speak with him. He asked if Scotty was considering attending Central Catholic, to which Scotty responded yes. The coach told Scotty, if he chose to come to Central Catholic, the coach would bring him in as a student manager. If he stuck with the program, he would earn a varsity letter.

John, Scotty, and I were impressed, recognizing how helpful this would be for Scotty in a large new school. He loved football, and since he had been unable to play, the opportunity to be team manager would allow him to be involved with a successful program. Scott's decision was made. CCHS was the best fit, with the best options. Somehow, we would manage. A scholarship, no matter the amount, would help.

Scholarship awardees were announced during the eighth-grade graduation program. We were more hopeful than optimistic. The first scholarship awarded was a one-year scholarship, the Schneider Memorial Scholarship. It was worth $1,000 awarded to one boy and one girl who would be attending a Catholic high school. When Scotty's name was called for this scholarship, it was difficult to suppress a scream. What made it more meaningful is that the scholarship was named after Carl Schneider, Scotty's fifth-grade teacher's husband. Scotty had received detention for calling her "the Devil." She was the first to hug him. He was not done receiving recognition. He won the Delp Family Scholarship worth $1,500 for his freshman year and $500 each subsequent year if he maintained a 3.00 GPA. This scholarship was given to a student from a South Toledo parochial school who chose CCHS. For this one, Scotty was competing against students from four schools.

More was still to come. Central Catholic also had scholarships to offer. As an incoming freshman, he was granted the Robert L. & Mary Francis Weisenburger Scholarship awarded to an OLPH student who attends CCHS. These grants put a huge dent in our first-year obligation. When you don't know how you can manage, resort to prayer. It worked for Scotty.

True to his word, the Toledo Central Catholic Football coach brought Scotty in as a team manager during summer practice and before his freshman year even began. What a great opportunity for Scotty. Freshman year in a centralized high school with students coming from all over the community can be intimidating. Even though Scotty could handle such a challenge, we still had some discomfort regarding how he might be accepted. Getting involved with the football players and related activities gave him an excellent chance to be more comfortable by the time school started. We knew Scotty's personality would win over the big guys.

Before he ever walked through the door to begin school, he was able to become acquainted with many football players, including upperclassmen. The coach's gesture and follow-through has never been forgotten. As summer practice was ending the day before school started, a big African American star tackle put his hand on Scotty's shoulder and said, "If anyone gives you any shit tomorrow, let us know!" A sentiment quickly echoed by other senior players. Nobody ever did: a credit to the school, the students, and the big tackle. Scotty stayed with the program the full four years, increasing his responsibilities to include videography breakdowns. He was now clearly Scott. His story was highlighted by a local TV sportscaster who broadcasted an interview with Scott and how he persevered. The highlight was his senior year, when the boys rolled through the season and won the Ohio State Division II state championship. He earned his varsity letter.

Being at CCHS for four years, we were bound to see funny Scotty surface. The most amusing was an assignment to care for a replica baby. The assignment was twenty-four-hour care for a computerized little "doll" baby. It was a pretty sophisticated doll that would cry and react much like an infant would during the period entrusted to his care. The baby could not be left unattended for too long or a demerit would be recorded. Demerits for other improper care would affect final grade. It even would wake overnight and need to be attended to. A darn good exercise for teenagers.

When Scott's turn came, the baby was placed in his arms at the end of class, and they were sent on their way. As he walked into the busy hallway during class change, a friend saw him, slapped him on the back, and sent the baby crashing into the lockers and tiled floor. Scott grabbed the baby and rushed back into the classroom to check with the teacher. And yes, the baby was dead, meaning an F within the first five minutes of care. The teacher did not want Scott to miss the benefit of this exercise, so he reset the baby and gave Scott a "mulligan."

He did an exceptional job caring for the baby. Since it could never be left unattended, we needed to take it with us when we went to visit my parents. Scott wanted to do something on the computer, so he set the little baby in a corner of a love seat in the loft. It was a safe and comfortable location near him. Unfortunately, my dad was overly intrigued by this thing and lifted it to examine. That was all right, but he rolled it around and tipped it upside down to check out some features. The baby screamed and cried. Dad quickly returned the baby to safety on the love seat. Scott said the only negative issue recorded was a period of excess roughhousing. Dad's curiosity cost him an "A."

Perhaps the most ridiculous lapse in judgment occurred when Scott was older and driving. Scott's good friend, Matt, had a collection of various traffic signs and related items. Scott, Matt, and friends were out tooling around when they came upon an old fire hydrant lying along the roadway. A new hydrant had been installed, and the old one had not been carted away yet. It was considered a valuable addition to Matt's collection. The boys managed to load the hydrant into Scott's car trunk, all while being observed by an off-duty sheriff's deputy. The deputy tried to show his badge and talk with them, but Scott avoided eye contact and drove away. When they arrived at Matt's house, they quickly got wisdom. Scott called John. We intentionally have deleted their conversation. John called the police department and asked them, "This is Officer John Noonan. Have you received a report about a missing fire hydrant?" The response was yes, one had been reported as being carried away by some boys. "Call off the search, I'm on it and will take care of it."

Every so often among his books, I would find a copy of *Maxim* magazine, a men's periodical. Once, I saw a $20 bill attached to a copy. I had a hunch he was going to send it in to pay for a subscription. Before I was able to say anything, he sent in cash. To this day, I am amazed that the person who processed the subscription did not pocket the money. They surely must have laughed knowing it was some teenager sneaking a subscription. He was just a typical teenage boy. My rule was any bikini photos and posters had to be on the inside of his closet door.

Scott performed well at CCHS. He maintained excellent grades, was well known, and active. Our decision to send him was validated over and over. His senior year, he was elected to the National Honor Society. The joy and pride I felt when he received his high school diploma are impossible to describe.

North to Alaska

With all he had sacrificed and suffered over the years, we wanted to do something unique and special as a graduation gift. The answer, a trip to Alaska—on his own. John's sister, Brenda, lives in Alaska, so we arranged for Scott to stay with her, her husband John, and family for ten days. This was something new for Scott and would prove to be an exciting adventure. He was put on a direct flight from Detroit to Anchorage. It was a nine-hour flight by himself. With a window seat, Scott was able to view all the mountainous scenery, which helped the miles and time fly by. I was a nervous wreck until I received a 3:00 a.m., our time, telephone call informing me that he was safe and with family.

Scott had the opportunity to fish in Alaskan waters. He was particularly taken by how they stowed the fish caught. In Ohio, fishermen are accustomed to taking bags of ice to preserve their catch. His uncle John simply steered the boat close to a "calving glacier" and chipped ice for their chest. Uncle John was in the military and gave him an American flag that had flown over a military base in Iran. Still one of his prized possessions. Scott's paternal grandparents, Barb and Jerry, made the trip to visit their daughter during his stay. For the trip highlight, they took a train to Denali National Park. Just more examples of how his adopted family embraced him. We worried less on his return flight since he was accompanied by Barb and Jerry. Scott casually mentioned he flew coach, and they got to fly first class.

Miami of Ohio

A college education was what we all believed Scott would need in order to fulfill his potential. He knew it and needed no prodding to further his education. We had been busy since his junior year in high school planning and evaluating colleges. As difficult as it was to release him to the world, we agreed he should go away for college. His top two choices were schools difficult to gain entry: the Ohio State University and Miami of Ohio. Interest in Ohio State was a given with his love for the Buckeyes. Miami of Ohio is described as a Public Ivy, being one of eight public universities evaluated as providing an education comparable to an Ivy League school. This made the school especially appealing. It's more compact—campus, size, and smaller community setting seemed ideal.

Scott applied to four schools and was admitted to all four: Ohio University, Bowling Green State University, the Ohio State University, and Miami of Ohio. It was now a choice between OSU and Miami. Both offered comparable scholarships and inducements, with Miami's overall cost actually being less. Miami offered him a special scholarship awarded to incoming freshmen who had overcome significant obstacles. In addition, he received a small book scholarship arranged by his former audiologist, Mrs. Kinker-Johnson. With the cost comparison resolved, it came down to preference. Miami's reputation and campus setting won. Living arrangements came next.

Scott was assigned to a 600 sq. feet quad dorm room. Meaning four freshmen, four carrel type study desks, closet/bureaus, and two stacked bunk beds in tight configuration. Scott had always enjoyed more privacy and security than this arrangement would provide. With all his scars and physical anomalies, it would be uncomfortable being with all new people. He was a trooper, though, and stuck it out for a full academic year. With less than ideal living arrangements favorable for studying, he attained a 3.00 GPA for his freshman year. No question he could compete on a collegiate level.

Early in his first year, we experienced a classic Scotty-ism. Because the room lacked privacy and security, the college recommended that students bring a small lockbox/safe. We bought him a Brink's lockbox to keep his important papers, credit card, and other valuable "stuff" secure. It would also help him avoid misplacing items. The box had a battery-operated electronic keypad for fast and easy access. It had a master key as backup in case the keypad did not work. The cause usually would be dead batteries, which can only be replaced by opening the lockbox. It came with two keys. Scott took one, and we kept one at home.

The stage is now set for the interesting exchange between John and Scott. He had been away at school only six weeks or so. At 10:00 a.m. on a Friday, John had come off his third shift patrol. He had been asleep for about ten minutes when the phone rang.

After a sleepy hello, the following conversation transpires:

Scott: Dad?
John: Yeah!

Scott: What?
John: Yes, Scott, it's me.

Scott: (*In a loud voice*) This stupid lockbox won't open…it's a piece of junk.
John: What are you talking about?

Scott: What?
John: (*In an agitated voice*) What are you talking about?

Scott: This stupid keypad on this stupid lockbox won't work.
John: What do you mean it won't work?

Scott: It won't open.
John: Are the LED lights coming on? Maybe you're using a wrong combination.

Scott: What?
John: Scott, can't you hear me?

Scott: Not well, my hearing aid battery is going dead.
John: (*Agitation increasing*) Then put in a new battery: I'll wait.

Scott: I can't…the batteries are in the lockbox… Is there any way to pick the lock?
John: (*At peak agitation*) Scott! It is specifically designed so you can't pick the lock or pry it open…the reason for having one.

Scott: This is just so stupid.
John: Scott, the keypad batteries are probably dead… Just open it with the key.

Scott: I can't.
John: Why not, did you lose the key already?

Scott: (*Insulted by the suggestion*) No, I did not lose the key.
John: Well, where is it?

Scott: You told me to put it someplace safe. It's in the lockbox.
John: How are you supposed to use the key if it's locked inside the box?

Scott: You told me to put it someplace safe… This is your fault, Dad.
John: Quiet! Don't say another word. I'll call you back when I figure out something.

What John figured out was to FedEx the key to Scott. Now awake, he took the backup key to a FedEx station. With assurance they could indeed overnight the key over the weekend to Oxford, Ohio, John gave them the key and delivery information. All was calm until he was told it would cost *$33*. Lucky for Scott, he was in Oxford. Scott did not know I had prepared for some problem like this and had placed a package of hearing aid batteries in his backpack. With Scott, I always needed to be one step ahead.

Final Years at Miami

His sophomore year, for his comfort and for better studying conditions, we moved Scott into a nice efficiency apartment close to campus. Scott now would have to be responsible for his own upkeep and cooking. We purchased everything he would need for housekeeping. Nice shiny new pots and pans nicely wrapped in cellophane, plus utensils. When we moved him back home three years later, pots, pans, and utensils were still in the original cellophane wrapping. Scott proved to be responsible living alone in an apartment and took school seriously. He barely missed graduating with honors, meaning he did exceptionally well after his freshman year.

Scott made the dean's list on numerous occasions, including one semester on the president's list.

The summer before leaving for college, Scott had gotten a job washing dishes for a local country club. It worked out so well he was able to work even over Christmas break and return each summer. Those may have been the last dishes he has washed. Scott was determined to graduate within a four-year period. To accomplish this, he needed to take one course over the summer between his junior and senior years. So he sacrificed his summer at home and dishwashing job to stay in Oxford. He kept his apartment and worked for the university maintenance department. He earned some needed money while completing the course he needed.

Scott to this day is a never-ending source of amusing anecdotes. He was becoming educated, but still present in him was the old Scotty. His last summer home from school, he was helping us by watching his younger brother. Josh was too young yet to stay alone. Josh was invited by a friend a few houses away to come and play. Scott gave him permission and set a time for Josh to come home. As one might expect, little boys cannot be counted on to adhere to a time to return home. Either they will not remember, or they will become so engaged they pay no attention to time.

So when Josh failed to return home, Scott strolled over to get him. As he approached the neighbor's house, he saw the neighbor with some others in their garage. The group was drinking beer and making fantasy football picks. Not one to pass up a chance to talk football, Scott grabbed a beer and joined them. After an hour, and likely another beer, Scott said, "Josh, we better be going." There was no Josh and had not been. Josh had actually gone home while Scott was in the neighbor's garage. While Scott was enjoying friendly conversation with the neighbors, Josh had been at home alone for the last hour.

Scotty became exceptionally organized and disciplined while in college. His history major required substantial reading, research, and papers. He developed a rigid schedule to ensure he would remain current with all his assignments. Missing class was never considered. This same attentiveness was applied to his daily life. He set a

MISS NANCY, UNCLE LARRY, AND A LIZARD NAMED KATHY

schedule of specific times to do each task, such as showering, eating, and laundry—when he did it. His Christmas wish one year was for everyone to give him boxers until he reached thirty pairs. Plenty of underwear would allow him to do laundry only monthly—a more frivolous example of his goal setting. Scott's organizational skill bordered on OCD.

After graduating from Miami, he carried his organizational skills and precise scheduling with him when he moved back home. His schedule was an annoyance to the rest of us living with him. We had developed our routine, and Scott brought his back home with him. Trying to blend him with the four of us and one bathroom was going to be a challenge. We provided him with privacy and space for himself. Blake, eleven, and Josh, seven, bunked together. If he had to leave early, he competed with us for the bathroom. I had a full-time job, so I needed my bathroom time too. Early mornings became hectic. One morning, I was finishing my makeup and hair. I could see Scott in the mirror's reflection standing behind me, staring. I asked him if he needed the sink and mirror to finish up. "Not yet." Puzzled, I asked, "What do you mean not yet?" He looked at me as if I should have known the reason. I could not believe his next words: "I brush my teeth at 7:03, and it's only 7:00."

Miami Graduation

Our Noonan Family at Christmas–2017
L–R: Blake, John, ME, Joshua, Scott

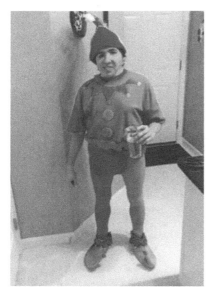

Scott's 27th Christmas

I want to be your Councilman

Scott with his Bacon Suit

Noonan, *"Present"*

Searching for Employment

Scott moving out became a goal for the whole family. College degree in hand, Scott now needed to find a job. Self-esteem, making your way in the world, paying back student loans, and moving into your own apartment requires a job. Scott found out what so many liberal arts grads discover—not many professional opportunities. He believed he would be a good fit in public service. With an undergraduate degree in history, he found it difficult to compete. He would have loved to work in a college athletic department in some capacity, for example, tutoring. He pursued positions at several colleges: OSU and Miami being preferred. He was constantly online checking athletic department postings in a four-state area. No luck.

His efforts in seeking employment were impressive and tireless. He would follow any lead he received and was constantly checking online for opportunities. It became frustrating for him. Failing to secure a job was not due to a lack of effort. He considered teaching. He took preparation courses to qualify and worked to be accepted on the substitute lists for four schools. Sub opportunities were sporadic. It was difficult for him to compete with those who were specifically trained as a teacher with the necessary subject major. He pretty much spent several days at a time babysitting a high school class. He made an effort to secure a position at Central Catholic where we believed he had the best chance.

After a year of erratic part-time work, a family acquaintance, the Lucas County auditor, asked Scott if he would like a six-month internship in her office. A good opportunity, even though it would be mostly computer clerical work. After being hired full-time when the internship ended, he worked four years in the auditor's office. During this time, he became acquainted with many county employees and officials and became active in the Lucas County Democratic Party.

With this position, Scott was able to move from home and get his own apartment. More importantly to Scott, he now had a steady income to start paying off his student loans. We got to move him one more time. Once again, we moved the same cellophane-wrapped pots, pans, and silverware and placing them in his new cupboard.

On the morning before he moved, I was finishing getting ready. I saw his reflection in the mirror standing again outside the bathroom door. I said to him mockingly, "It's not 7:03 yet." He was less than amused and said he had a question. "When I finally do move out, what exactly are you and Dad going to pay for?" I laughed. Laughed and looked him straight on and, while pointing to my lips like I used to when he was little, loudly said, "Nothing!"

He became active in political campaigns and gained a reputation as a tireless worker. Scott volunteered for civic and social issues. He now had what he needed to obtain a professional career position: a positive reputation and great contacts. His big break came when two professional positions became available simultaneously—one being an administrative position within the Lucas County Probate Court. Through his political and civic involvement, he had developed a relationship with presiding Judge Puffenberger, the judge who had guided Scott's adoption. It was a good reconnection for Scott. The judge offered him a position. He had also interviewed with the United Way of Greater Toledo.

When he was offered the United Way position, Scott had to make a choice. After years seeking a career job, he had two offers to consider. He felt loyalty to Judge Puffenberger, but believed the UW position would offer more opportunity. To his credit, Judge Puffenberger supported Scott taking the UW position.

Thoughts from Scott

At a family function, Blake interviewed Scott as our entertainment. We expected to get some laughs, as those two together make quite an entertaining act. He was mostly serious.

Blake: What is your earliest childhood memory?
Scott: Falling face-first into a bowl of Spaghettios.

Blake: Who are some people outside of family who had significantly affected your life?

Scott: Bob Johnson, Anita Lopez, she gave me my first career-directed job. Coach Greg Dempsey and so many at OLPH and Central Catholic.

Blake: What do you remember about living in an apartment?
Scott: I still do.

Blake: Come on, I mean as a little kid.
Scott: Sorry, you needed to be more specific. Had my own room, Super Nintendo, long driveway, and inconvenient parking, and the swimming pool.

Blake: Did you have a favorite stuffed animal?
Scott: Rodney, little stuffed bear with one ear missing and wearing an OSU T-shirt. He was always with me in the hospital and always got his own wristband like mine.

Blake: Who were your childhood role models?
Scott: Mom and Dad.

Blake: What good time stands out growing up?
Scott: Going to Indians ball games with my mom.

Blake: Who are you most like in the family?
Scott: Mom when I was younger, Dad as I got older. But I have always been wise.
Blake: (*Under his breath*) Bull.

Blake: What has been most difficult for you to deal with?
Scott: Hearing issues: ear infections, wearing a hearing aid difficult to keep in place. Initially fought the BAHA. It is a life changer.

Blake: After all the surgeries, what are you still not able to do you would like to do?

Scott: Being able to turn my neck fully left and right. Would have liked to have been able to join the military.

Blake: What was your first job?
Scott: Food service at the Toledo Zoo. Hated working with the food, but liked working the counter.

Blake: Did you ever feel as though life has been unfair to you?
Scott: No, never. Always had fun. Never picked on or bullied. Able to get an education.

Blake: Why do you think you were never bullied?
Scott: My personality for one thing. Always someone to defend me. Had friends who would eliminate any problem.

Blake: What made you think breaking the garage door window to get in the locked house would be okay?
Scott: It was the most efficient way to get in.

Blake: Why Miami vs. Ohio State?
Scott: Smaller school and walkable campus. Just felt better.

Blake: How do you wish life could have been different?
Scott: Things could have been easier with no limitations.

Blake: Any regrets?
Scott: The silly things I did when little, like breaking the garage door window.

Blake: Did you ever get detention?
Scott: Caught practicing Mom's signature to forge. Calling Mrs. Schneider the devil. She taught religion.

EPILOGUE

In reading this story, one should appreciate how it was possible for Scott to evolve into the man he is today. It took a mother who fought to have him mainstreamed. It took some concessions by a good school system and educators. It took a young boy who refused to fall prey to "woe is me." It was instinctive in Scott to work hard, and by engaging people and embracing life, he knew he could make something of himself.

They were helped on the journey by numerous people who came into their lives at the right time with the right sensitivities. Initially, it was a loving family, followed by a loving and caring adoptive father and his parents and family. Included were savvy school administrators, caring social agency personnel, safety net programs for disabled children, Shriner's International, the kindness of strangers, and Scott himself.

Scott's Hero Bench is full of people who at some point made a difference.

Scott's Heroes:

- Sue Schramm Wonsetler: school principal
- Mrs. Smith and Mrs. Laubenthal: first teachers
- Joyce Kinker-Johnson, MA, CCC-A (audiologist)
- Dave Jones: first Little League coach
- Dr. E. O. Kelley (DDS, deceased)
- Dr. Peter Smith, orthopedic surgeon and staff at Shriners Children's Hospital
- Father Jim Halleron

- o Dr. Joseph Schneider (PCP, deceased)
- o Dr. Larry Winegar (ENT, retired)
- o Kathy Dusseau, Our Lady of Perpetual Help/St. Rose
- o Honorable Jack Puffenberger, presiding judge, Lucas Co. Probate Court
- o Fr. Joe Steinbauer
- o Greg Dempsey: Toledo Central Catholic head football coach
- o GOD

At this writing in 2018, Scott is the *labor engagement liaison for the United Way of Greater Toledo*: a full-time position. He is serving a term as a *Maumee City councilman*. No individual efforts of others or sacrifices by Scott were wasted. He is paying back the community through his selfless political activity and volunteer participation. Scott's civic and volunteer activities are as follows:

Civic and Community Groups:

- o SmithFest registration chair
- o Toledo-Lucas County Commission on Disabilities board member
- o Lucas County Board of Developmental Disabilities member
- o Ohio Theater and Events Committee member
- o Promise House Project treasurer
- o Fair Housing Committee member
- o Toledo Police Athletic League treasurer
- o Fraternal Order of Eagles member
- o Northwest Ohio Labor Fest treasurer
- o Labor Memorial Day Committee member
- o Labor Day Parade Committee member
- o Labor Loves the Library Committee member
- o UT Phi Kappa Phi alumni affiliate
- o YWCA I Rise Committee member
- o Latino Alliance member
- o Coalition of Black Trade Unionists member
- o NAACP Toledo Chapter member

Political Groups:

- ○ Lucas County Young Democrats events coordinator
- ○ South Toledo Dems secretary
- ○ Maumee Dems
- ○ African American Leadership Caucus member
- ○ Lucas County Democratic Party Executive Committee

City of Maumee:

- ○ City Councilman
- ○ Building and Lands/Land Use and Zoning Committees chair
- ○ Code, Finance and Economic Development Committee member
- ○ Parks and Recreation, and Water and Sewer Committees member
- ○ Toledo Metropolitan Area Coalition of Governments member
- ○ Maumee Chamber of Commerce city member

More chapters to this young life will be written. We cannot wait to read them.

Epilogue written by Gus Finorky, family friend

Author Listing

Writers:
Betsy Noonan
David Stratso

Contributors:
Mary Lu Stratso
Nancy Szczublewski
Cynthia Bojarski
Blake Noonan

Cover Design:
Blake Noonan

Title:
Joseph Bojarski

John's Family

My Family

John's Family

- Jerry and Barb Noonan, parents
  - John and Betsy
    Scott
    Blake
    Joshua

  - Brenda and John Snelson, sister and brother-in-law
    Cassandra
    William

  - Jeff and Amy, brother and sister-in-law
    Averi
    Garrett

  - Bonnie Noonan, sister: not pictured (RIH October 7, 2018)

My Family

- Dave and Mary Lu Stratso, my parents
  - Nancy and Greg Szczublewski, sister and brother-in-law
    Corey, son and wife Angela, little Hank and little Jay
    Kyle, son and wife, Sara
    Casey, son

  - Cynthia and Joseph Bojarski, sister and brother-in-law
    Christian, son

ABOUT THE AUTHOR

Betsy Noonan grew up in Perrysburg, Ohio. While raising a family of three boys along with her husband John, she has worked full-time for most of her adult life. Her twenty-eight-year career has been in real estate title work evolving into real estate sales. She is the middle child of three sisters. Her engaging personality and resourcefulness became her weapon in seeking the complexity of help needed for her firstborn.

David Stratso is a retired human resource professional. He is a graduate of the Ohio State University with a BSBA in industrial relations. The majority of his career was at the corporate level with a major Toledo-based Fortune 500 corporation. Following early retirement, he continued working in HR consulting, and brief periods as HR director with the former Medical College of Ohio and a manufacturing/engineering company in Bowling Green, Ohio, before fully retiring in 1999.